NEIGHBOURS

NEIGHBOURS

*Subdivision Life in England
and the United States*

by

H. E. BRACEY

BATON ROUGE
LOUISIANA STATE UNIVERSITY PRESS

CONTENTS

Contents

Contents

TABLES

PREFACE

THE following pages derive from a survey begun on new housing estates near Bristol, England, in 1957 and continued on a number of new subdivisions near Columbus, Ohio, in 1958 and 1959. The enquiry was designed to study the adjustment of (mainly) urban families to life in new rural–urban fringe neighbourhoods. As far as we know, it is the first household survey of its kind to attempt a comparison of the way of life of such families in the two countries, which are separated by three thousand miles of sea yet speak the same language, almost, and think of themselves, often, as being so alike but are in fact, as we shall see, frequently, so different.

I am Chairman of the South Gloucestershire Committee of the Gloucestershire Community Council, which, for American readers, I should explain is a voluntary body, found in most English counties, whose main function is to encourage, co-ordinate and develop the social well-being and activities of the mainly rural inhabitants within its territory. Through my connection with this body I was acutely aware that many newcomers on new estates in Bristol's rural–urban fringe were only imperfectly adjusting themselves to the life of the neighbourhoods in which they found themselves; there was loneliness amongst the women, too few organizations existed for teenagers and so on. In 1957, I was joined at the University of Bristol, England, by Merton D. Oyler, of the Ohio State University, U.S.A., who wished to spend a Sabbatical six months on some kind of social research. A study on one or two peripheral estates seemed to be worth while.

An interview outline (see Appendix A) was devised and interviews were taken in the homes of a sample of householders selected on a random basis. It was later decided to increase the number of interviews to 120, and, if possible, to carry out the same number in new neighbourhoods around Columbus, Ohio, choosing subdivisions where the residents were, as near as possible, comparable by income and social status. Sub-sequently, Walter V. Babics of the Department of Sociology, the Ohio State University, continued the interviews in America and A. H. Scarrott, Area Officer of the Gloucestershire Community Council, those in England.

In 1959, the University of Bristol granted me leave of absence to spend six months in America, where I assisted with the interviewing and acquired valuable background information. As the work proceeded, I became especially interested in the contrasts in the way of life in the two countries and particularly in the pattern of 'neighbouring' as I have termed it. It is this aspect I have treated in detail in the book; information and data from other parts of the enquiry are used only as background to this main theme.

My thanks are due in the first place, of course, to Dr. Oyler, who convinced me that the project was worth starting, who carried through the first interviews in England and later persuaded me to join him in the United States. The original material on which this book is based is part of a larger collection assembled jointly by Dr. Oyler and me. Its publication here does not preclude Dr. Oyler from drawing on the same material for analysis. Local authorities, voluntary organizations and the residents in both countries co-operated admirably. I would like to express appreciation of the time and effort they so unstintingly placed at our disposal.

I am grateful to Dr. Babics and Mr. Scarrott, who shared the interviewing, especially for their skill and patience in obtaining the co-operation of householders so successfully.

I must also put on record my thanks to the two universities, the University of Bristol, England, and the Ohio State University, United States of America, for the facilities which were made available to enable the project to be carried through. In America, the Bureau of Educational Research and Service provided grants of money which enabled Dr. Oyler to finance the interviewing in America; I am grateful especially to the interest shown by Dr. Nisonger, Director of the Bureau. The Gloucestershire Community Council readily agreed that its Area Officer should carry out interviews in England.

The manuscript was read by many friends in both countries.

They are too numerous to mention individually and I would thank them here for the help their comments afforded me. One I must name, my colleague Professor H. D. Dickinson of the University of Bristol, who has read most of the manuscripts I have brought to the point of publication. As before, his comments were penetrating and his criticism fair: oftentimes they made me question statements which had seemed unquestionable.

I have hinted already that the two peoples do not quite speak the same language. This early gave rise to some difficulty in preparing a publication acceptable in both countries. For instance, throughout I have used the awkward (to an English ear) terms 'low-cost' or 'low-priced' when referring to 'cheap' housing because 'cheap' in American usage carries an undertone suggesting poor value for money. Satisfactory substitutions for other words which might prove ambiguous have not always been available: where misunderstanding was likely I have included a 'translation' in brackets in the text until it was reasonable to assume the reader had become familiar with this addition to, or variant from, his vocabulary: thus salesman (commercial traveller). At this point it should be explained that the words 'estate' in England and 'subdivision' in the United States have not identical meanings. A building 'estate' is an area of land acquired for development mainly by one builder. A 'subdivision', on the other hand, is an area of land which may or may not have been acquired by a single realtor (estate agent); but the actual building operations may be undertaken by a score of builders.

Finally, I cannot assess too highly the part played by my wife in the work. In America, she set up home on a post-war subdivision and did her best to enable us to live as an 'ordinary' American couple: in this she was ably assisted by Mrs. Betty Oyler. My wife attended all the visits made to homes for the purpose of interviewing, and many others besides. This frequently meant setting out at 7 p.m. and returning past midnight. The 'formal' part of the interview, which was taken on a tape recorder, was almost invariably followed by 'socializing', as our American friends would describe it; in other words, in getting to know the family better. This took the form of conversing with any other members of the family who were on hand—and often friends who had been invited to 'drop in to meet the British', for news of our visits travelled quickly around the subdivisions. As the interviewing programme proceeded our welcome became noticeably increasingly cordial. We were invited by the proud owners to admire every detail of the new home and its furnishings, to examine the new equipment, the air conditioner or the attic fan, the kitchen-waste destructor or the dish-washer, the garage doors operated by an infra-red ray and so on. The morning after each interview my wife and I gave to playing back the previous day's recordings and recalling details of our experiences and conversations with the family: the information we transferred to our prepared schedules. This 'conference' was essential, for often whilst I had been appraising the husband's do-it-yourself efforts in the basement, my wife had been 'visiting with' (an American expression meaning holding friendly conversation) the wife in the bedroom. Altogether, we shared a memorable experience for which we count ourselves fortunate.

HOWARD E. BRACEY

University of Bristol

Postscript

The galley proofs and most of the page proofs were received by me whilst I was serving as Visiting Professor in the Department of Sociology at Louisiana State University. Thus, the final corrections to the text were made when my wife and I were once more 'living as Americans' in an apartment in Baton Rouge. Furthermore, I had been able to 'try out' the script on several American audiences and groups of friends. I must thank our friends, especially Al Bertrand and Lee Taylor, at Louisiana State University for their help in this regard.

H. E. B.

I

THE PEOPLE

Our Neighbours

WE found that most English householders are quite ready to talk about themselves and their neighbours—in fact, many appeared to gain some satisfaction in doing so. By contrast, American respondents were not especially forthcoming about themselves and showed a certain reluctance in talking about their neighbours; at first, we had to draw them out concerning differences they had noticed although the majority eventually lost their early diffidence in this respect, For example, many Americans asserted, quite wrongly, as we shall show, that their neighbours were in the same circumstances, and acted in the same way, as they themselves. It soon became clear to us that this was not due to lack of observation or inadequate knowledge on their part, but to the strong streak of conformity observable in most Americans. Let us look first at some of the American replies taken from the taped interviews:

'We are all young people with lots of kids. We all have to wait until pay-day to buy something.' It was in these terms that a working-man, living in one of the least-expensive houses, described himself and his neighbours. How wrong people can be in their assessment of others around them! On this subdivision[1] we found that in the sample of twenty families, two had one child, eight had two and six had three children. Only two

---

[1] Throughout the text, in order to reduce the number of references to the two countries of which we write, the word 'subdivision' is used to describe a new American, and the word 'estate' a new English, housing development.

families had four or more children, which might, perhaps, be described as 'lots of kids'. The ages of the husbands ranged from 22 years to 49 years and their wives from 20 years to 47 years, the average being 31 years for husbands and 29 years for wives. The incomes of this man's neighbours, based on 'take-home' pay, varied from $3,600 (£1,281) to $8,700 (£3,096) per annum: a fair range. As for 'waiting for pay-day', this was difficult to check but, admittedly, most of the young ones were struggling to pay off their instalments on the car, the storm windows, refrigerator or other items of household equipment.

Next we have the assessment of a salesman (commercial traveller) earning $6,600 (£2,357) living in one of the inter-mediate-priced houses on a subdivision where occupations varied very markedly indeed. He could not say that his neigh-bours were all doing the same job so he tried to generalize and make them fit the mould by saying, 'Most of us are factory workers, salesmen or white-collar workers. We are all in the same income bracket.' This is a wide enough range of occupa-tion, in all conscience. Nearby was a cabinet-maker earning $6,000 (£2,140) a year: 'We all have a house full of kids.' All 'good' Americans are supposed to like and have a lot of children; this is the public image of themselves they have projected through-out the United States and abroad through their magazines, films and television programmes. This tradesman had two children. 'All have bills to pay,' said another; we later learned from him that the contract on his two-year-old Dodge, parked on the drive, had one more year to run before the final instal-ment was paid. He was probably thinking of this.

Even where it was fairly obvious that the people living round about were different from our informants, attempts were made, repeatedly, to see the same qualities in the neighbours as they themselves possessed. Thus a car mechanic on the lowest-priced subdivision found that 'People are all trying to get ahead'. He himself was doing very well and, with hard work and long hours, was bringing home $8,000 (£2,847) a year at the age of thirty. Another, a young man of 21 years living on a medium-priced subdivision, earning the low wage (for the United States) of $4,000 (£1,424) a year, as a clerk, had not gone on to college when he graduated from high school. But

2

he was attending night-school classes (twilight courses) and hoped eventually to obtain a university degree. His comment, that 'People (his neighbours) are graduates mostly', reflected his ambition rather than the facts of the situation; our sample gave us six male and three female graduates out of 40 adults in the 20 households in his subdivision group. His neighbour was more honest and recognized differences but he, too, felt impelled to explain that 'There is no regard paid to income levels. I may drive a Cadillac and they a beaten-up Ford. . . . You take others as they are. . . . I value this highly. . . . They are the least money-conscious community we have ever lived in.' (In fact this family ran two Fords—one two and the other six years old.) But were they less money-conscious? Our evidence seemed not to support this. Was this another piece of church, magazine, T.V. or radio 'propaganda'—of image building?

This apparent desire of the American people we met to conform was one of our early surprises. It was much less evident on the highest-priced subdivisions, and even on the others it must be stated that a minority were prepared to say that their neighbours differed from them and each other in income, general outlook and way of life. The following descriptions given by three of this American minority might almost be English in the recognition of class barriers:

'Our street had the largest down payment of the three and this makes a difference in the type of families. The third street of this project is very low. The second street has a lot of feuds over their children.' Another, a woman school-teacher, said quite simply: 'I live between two working people and don't have coffee breaks with them.' Her near neighbour described the social status of his neighbours quite neatly with: 'I never saw any neighbour with a golf-club in his hand.'

The quotations, above, have all been from occupiers of homes on 'projects', i.e. subdivisions comprising low-cost houses. On the higher-priced subdivisions there was sometimes an acute awareness of the difference in neighbours and markedly less reticence to state this fact: it was not, however, based on differences of education as might have been expected. Thus, one householder, a stonemason, reflected and summarized the remarks of his neighbours in the following: 'Everybody is

3

represented, I'd say: lawyers, real-estate salesmen, radio broad-caster, insurance, factory workers, stonemason.' The reasons for this wide range he adduced from the fact that the development was not a 'project' where homes were alike and purchase price sorted out the type of people. On his subdivision large lots (plots in the English usage) of one acre were available: this he argued selected people who were 'mostly the energetic type'. Many had built or part-built their homes (houses in English usage). A greater occupational and social range had resulted. In this he was correct and we shall see that these facts affected the kind of neighbouring which took place.

Whilst residence on most American subdivisions is selective, in so far as income determines the initial deposit and therefore the type of house and locality which is chosen, a greater mixing of people of different age, incomes and occupations existed. In England, the social gulf between the council house (public housing) and the private-enterprise estate is marked and is recognized by both sides. Let us take first the council estate. Many council-house tenants we interviewed betrayed feelings of inferiority as to income and education; they were often at pains to explain that their relatively low income and/or occu-pational status was due to missed or absent educational facilities when they were younger; this many hoped to remedy for their offspring. The majority of council-house tenants tended to accept the handicap of inadequate education (as they viewed it) as a fact of life, and few gave evidence that they were striving to 'better themselves' either by further education or by saving up a deposit for a house of their own. This must not be taken to be the view of all working-class persons. Many 'brighter' people of working-class origin had, without doubt, obtained their own accommodation on private-enterprise estates, in older houses or had been fortunate to secure rented accom-modation. Only four of all our private-enterprise householders had been tenants of council houses, 'Why should we buy?' council tenants would ask. They were occupying accommoda-tion subsidized by the State to the tune of about £50 a year. Their present living conditions were vastly superior to what most had been used to: 'There is a very nice class of people up here. It's not rowdy. You don't get the Saturday night rowdies

4

shouting through the streets.' Or, 'They are all like the average working-man, not many of them have got office jobs.'

Council tenants, then, showed themselves content with their lot—or at least most did and there was seldom any suggestion that this house was a stepping-stone to something better. They pointed out to us that, in general, getting a council house on a new estate is regarded with envy by other working-class people: 'People in Bristol say, "Oh you live with the nobs. You must have plenty of money to live there."' This is a reference to the urban fringe situation of these new council estates, which involves the family in higher transport costs, and to the fact that rents tend to be some 18s. 0d. ($2.52) a week higher than for council houses within the city boundary. With two exceptions, all the council tenants interviewed were very happy with conditions as they found them. 'You know it's a council estate but it doesn't look like one. The lay-out is good and the houses are not packed out' was how one described the attractive designs and convenient planning of the estate. Side by side with this satisfaction was a feeling of surprise, sometimes bewilderment, that people could be so different from what they had expected, or from those they had mixed with in the old, congested, downtown areas from which most had come. 'The people are all the same round here. All the people are *respectable*. There's a woman round the corner that's got seven boys and you *never* hear her swear at them.'

But, as in America, not all streets are peopled by the same kind of persons, or at least so it seems to the people who live in them. 'The other side of the pub seems rougher.' 'The best people live on the edge of the estate (where they lived). Some let the place down.' Or, more charitably, 'They are rough-and-ready on the other part of the estate.' In both countries, there seems to be a loyalty to one's immediate neighbours; the people amongst whom you live and whom you know seem friendlier, their houses appear cleaner, and their gardens look tidier, than those at the other end of the road—unless there is a real defaulter.

The general feeling about people round about them on English private-enterprise estates was well summed up by the head of one family: 'It's quiet here. There is no rowdyism. The people are nice to know. Most families seem to be young.' The wife added, 'We like being with young people. We've all got something in common.' These sentiments were expressed, in different words, by many householders, but it was not meant to imply that everyone lived a jolly life together, for this would not have been true. Variations in education, income and ways of life, were recognized and behaviour adjusted accordingly. 'They are a very mixed crowd . . . very nice I think. Some have come to get settled before retirement.' 'They are a mixed bunch with diverse characters in every way. There are low-class and better-class. The low-class are trying to ape their betters.' It should be explained that this last man was enjoying a higher income than most of his neighbours and was at cross-purposes with his next-door neighbour. A young commercial traveller (salesman), newly-arrived from another city, described his new neighbourhood as '. . . a very mixed community here. Some are starving to pay for their homes and this tends to make them unhappy and unsociable.'

The English private-enterprise estates, like the more-expensive American subdivisions studied, were peopled mainly by professional people. Nevertheless, at least a quarter of the English private-enterprise householders could be described as artisans. They appeared to mix well enough with their professional neighbours and no feuds or jealousies were uncovered, but a certain bravado could sometimes be detected in their replies. For example, an artisan, a maintenance engineer, asserted that 'nearly all are working-class people here. You don't have to live up to directors and executives around here.' Then, rather inconsistently, he added, 'There is a school-teacher next door and he has a better job than I have but he works like me.' In spite of this protestation of equality, this man had wasted two years before daring to don his shorts to work in the garden; then he only did so when he observed his neighbour exposing his knees on a particularly hot day. He explained to us that he waited so long because 'I didn't want to let the neighbourhood down'.

This convention, that the neighbourhood had to be lived up to, came to light continually on all council and private-enterprise estates in England. With it went the fear that you might inadvertently let yourself down in the eyes of the neighbours and the neighbourhood.

Husbands and Wives: Age

The average age of all American husbands interviewed was 36 years and that of their wives 34 years (Table 1). The corresponding ages of English husbands and wives was 35·5 years and 33·5 years, respectively. Thus, for both countries, the ages of husbands and wives were comparable; in both, wives were, on average, two years younger than their spouses.

TABLE I

Average Age of Persons Interviewed
U.S.A. and England

Estate or Subdivision	U.S.A.		England	
	Husband	Wife	Husband	Wife
A	31	29	30·5	29
B	31·5	30	32·5	30·5
C	36	33	34	32
D	33	33	42·5	40
E	43	42	38·5	37
F	42	39	35	33
All	36 yrs.	34 yrs.	35·5 yrs.	33·5 yrs.

Subdivision A comprised the lowest-cost houses; house values (by purchase price) increased through B, C, D, E to F which contained the highest-cost houses.

Estates A, B and C comprised council houses.

The average age of householders in English council houses (estates A, B, C) was five years or so lower than those occupying higher-cost, private-enterprise houses. In America, the occupiers of the highest-priced houses (subdivisions E and F) were, on average, over 40 years of age, i.e. some ten or twelve years older than those in the lowest-cost houses (subdivisions A and B).

7

Children

The overall average number of children in American families was 2·0 and in English families was 1·7. But these figures take no account of childless families or those with married children in our samples. In both countries, three households had married children living away from, and no others living at, home; the average for both countries was 2·0 children for each of these families.

But, in America there were 9, and in England 19, childless households out of a total of 120 in each country. Since the adult average age for the two national samples differed only slightly, the considerable contrast, 7·5 per cent for America and 15·8 for England, reflects the earlier age at which a young American couple begins to raise a family.

The average number of children in families where there were children living at home was 2·2 and 1·9 for America and England respectively (Table 2). American houses are not teeming with children as some Americans would have us believe.

TABLE 2

Average Number of Children

Estate or Subdivision	Children per family with children at home		Families without children		Families without children at home but with children living away	
	U.S.A.	England	U.S.A.	England	U.S.A.	England
A	2·4	1·3	1	4	0	0
B	2·2	2·0	1	1	0	1
C	2·8	2·1	3	4	0	0
D	2·0	2·1	3	2	1	1
E	2·0	2·2	2	6	1	1
F	2·0	1·9	2	5	1	0
Total	2·2	1·9	12	22	3	3

Occupations

The occupations of householders interviewed are summarized for the two countries in Table 3. The two lists appear broadly comparable by occupation, although it is difficult to make an

TABLE 3

Occupations of Householders

Category	Occupation	U.S.A.	England
1	Building workers	11	11
2	Electrical technicians	4	5
3	Transport workers (wage-earners) incl. postmen	4	9
4	Other technicians (mainly engineering)	28	38
5	Salesmen (incl. commercial travellers and firms' representatives)	15	11
6	Clerical workers (incl. shop assistants)	11	12
7	Educational employees (teachers and professors)	7	3
8	Professional engineers	11	6
9	Other higher professional workers	18	8
10	Self-employed persons	2	4
11	Retired, widowed and divorced persons	3	7
12	Miscellaneous	6	6
Total persons		120	120

accurate assessment when the description 'engineer' was frequently given for both professional and manual operatives. From the table the proportion of manual workers in the English sample appears to be slightly higher than in the United States. The number of persons with higher educational attainment and/or special skills was twice as many in the American sample, however, if this is measured by the sum of persons in categories 7–9, i.e. 36 persons to 17. The figure for salesmen (commercial travellers) in the United States subdivisions, i.e. 15, is high by comparison with the English total of 10.

Somewhat surprisingly the number of wives who went out to

work was almost identical for both countries and comprised 20 per cent and 19 per cent for America and England, respectively. No significant variation in this proportion with income was noticeable in either country and the average of 4 out of 20 working housewives held good for all subdivisions and estates.

Household Outgoings

The income of householders living on the cheapest American subdivision was of the order of $6,000 and on the higher-priced ones around $10,000 per annum (i.e. £2,140 and £3,560, respectively). The corresponding figures in England were £600 and £900 per annum (i.e. $1,690 and $2,530, respectively). These figures give some indication of the higher level of remuneration in the United States of America: they do not take into account the cost of living difference in the two countries.

Half the English householders were council tenants and occupied houses or flats (apartments) which cost a little under £2,000 (i.e. $5,620) each to build. The lowest-cost American, project houses were bought at $12,000 (i.e. £4,271). The price of private-enterprise houses in England ranged from £2,100 to just under £3,000 (i.e. $5,901 and $8,430, respectively). The highest-priced American homes, on average, ranged from $25,000 (i.e. £8,897) to $35,000 (i.e. £12,456). All English houses were brick-built; all American houses were constructed of timber although some employed a stone 'veneer' for parts of their exterior walls.

It is impossible to give a very accurate average of household outgoings on such items as mortgage repayments, house insurance and rates and taxes since the modes of purchase and payment varied so widely. Only one or two occupiers had paid cash; a few had secured an overdraft from the bank; others had effected their house purchase through a life assurance policy. Nevertheless, it can be said that the great majority of house owners in both countries were buying their houses by means of a mortgage advance from a building (and loan) society (association). Some American agreements allowed the mortgagee to pay off lump sums, large or small, at his discretion. These irregular payments are ignored in our averages, below, which are based only on those where *regular* repayment of capital and/or interest were paid; this represented three-quarters of all householders interviewed in America and 96·7 per cent in England.

American repayments ranged from $900 (i.e. £320) per annum approximately, including local taxes. The average house repayments by council tenants in England amounted to £110 (i.e. $309) and by owner-occupiers £150 (i.e. $422), the average, overall English repayments amounted to £125 (i.e. $351); both figures include local rates; the council-house tenant has not to meet payments for outdoor decorating and structural repairs and maintenance. From these figures it would appear that Americans were paying out in house rent or repayments approximately 14½ per cent of their total income (take-home pay) compared with the Englishman's 16 per cent. The difference of only one and a half per cent is small; in fact, the gap may be slightly wider than this since the American house purchase price, which determines repayments, includes such items as central heating furnace, refrigerator and cooking range. These items are provided separately by the English purchaser and where he entered into hire purchase agreements for them they should, for true comparison, have been added to his regular outgoings; detailed information concerning hire purchase commitments was not sought at the interview. Furthermore, the American taxes, which have been added to the house mortgage here, included sizeable sums towards the upkeep of local services including the school system. In England, a much larger proportion of the cost of local education is borne by the taxpayer from central government funds. This is not included in our calculations above.

Since English heating systems are generally less efficient, and fuel is relatively much more expensive, a greater proportional outlay on heating would be expected. In fact, it was found that, adding the outgoings on coal, gas, oil and electricity for each household, the Englishman spent, on average, £51 ($142) compared with the American's $270 (£96) (Table 4); in other words the cost of cooking, heating and lighting was twice as much for the American householder—not so great a burden considering

TABLE 4

Annual Outlay on Coal, Gas and/or Electricity per Household

Estate or Subdivision	Annual Outlay				Number of Returns in the Analysis	
	England		U.S.A.		England	U.S.A.
	£ s d.	$	$	£ s. d.		
A	52 16 0	148^{40}	241^{40}	86 0 0	13	18
B	48 14 0	136^{80}	213^{20}	75 18 0	20	18
C	39 9 0	122^{00}	218^{20}	77 14 0	8	18
D	52 4 0	146^{70}	243^{70}	86 14 0	19	15
E	56 6 0	158^{20}	317^{50}	113 0 0	15	15
F	48 16 0	137^{00}	386^{90}	137 12 0	17	18
Total	£50 16 0	$\$142^{80}$	$\$269^{50}$	£96 0 0	92	102

that the latter's average income was three to four times that of his English opposite number.

There is only a slight correlation, in Table 4, between the type of house and its outlay on fuel. It is true, however, that the smallest outgoings of fuel occurred in England on a council estate (C) and on one of the lowest-priced projects (B). The largest outgoings on fuel in England were on a private-enterprise estate (F), and in the United States on the highest-priced housing development (F); this last was in part because piped gas was not available and oil-fired furnaces had had to be installed.[1]

Transport

All but two American families owned an automobile: one was a widow and the other an old-age pensioner: none owned motor-cycles. In England, 43 per cent of all householders interviewed owned or had the sole use of a motor-car, whilst another 15 per cent owned a motor-cycle, making a total of 58 per cent

[1] The cost of running an oil-fired furnace in Columbus, Ohio, was approximately twice that of operating a gas-fired system.

with a mechanically-propelled vehicle. On the English private-enterprise estates, 80 per cent had the sole use of a car, a figure which will probably surprise many people on both sides of the Atlantic.

No English but exactly one-quarter of all American households ran a second car. Except a handful, all these were found on the three highest-priced subdivisions. Two families ran a third car.

In both countries, the primary use to which the family car was put was to take the breadwinner to work; father had first call on the family car in one-car families. In England, the family car was occasionally reserved for weekends and holiday motoring: in the United States never.

TABLE 5

The Journey to Work: Means of Transport used by Householders (as per cent of total)

	U.S.A.	England
Private transport (car/motor-cycle)	84	49
Car pool	10	4
Private hired (bus)	0	5
Public transport	2	15
Walk or bicycle	2	25
Not working	2	2
Owning car	99	53
Owning motor-cycle	0	18

From Table 5 it will be seen that 84 per cent of American, compared with 49 per cent English, workers usually journeyed to work by means of private car or motor-cycle. A further 10 per cent American, and 4 per cent English, workers shared a car pool which makes the two proportions 94 per cent and 53 per cent, respectively.

Generalizing, all but half a dozen Americans, but only a half of all Englishmen, travelled to work by private car or motor-cycle. A quarter of English male householders used their feet either in walking or pedalling a bicycle; 15 per cent used public transport (compared with only 2 per cent of Americans); a further 5 per cent shared the cost of hiring a special bus to take them to and from the aircraft factory.

Bus services were a favourite object of abuse in both countries. In England 32 per cent, and in the United States 23 per cent, of all householders passed some complaint against the bus service or the bus company. These came especially from the lower-paid workers. The better-off residents in England had cars to use and in America a second car to leave at home for the wife to use. In America it was the wife and not the husband who complained about 'The city bus. It's terrible, it really is!' Another: 'There are no buses out here at all. It sure does tie you down with two children.' The nearest bus-stop from these two subdivisions was ten or fifteen minutes' walk away—not an excessive distance by English standards. They were one-car families where the husband had not joined a car pool for the journey to work, perhaps because he needed the car throughout the day for his work, for example as salesman or service mechanic. The women were looking forward with confidence to the not very distant future when the household would have a second car, often acquired by not trading in the present car when buying a new one. Most American women hold driving licences: car-driving and car maintenance lessons are on the curriculum of most high schools. It is very convenient for the family when the 16-year-old firstborn reaches the senior-high class and gets ready to take his driving test;[1] having passed this he can take the younger members of the family to school and relieve his mother of the duty she has performed, or shared with a neighbour, daily, for the past ten years. Schools are having to construct larger and still-larger parking lots to accommodate the 'hot rods' of their senior pupils; father usually has too much sense to allow his son to drive the family car except when supervised, and the car the teenager drives is frequently acquired from a well-to-do friend who is 'turning in' an old car, or from a nearby sales lot using money earned during vacations and weekends whilst serving in shops, working in a factory or cutting

[1] In some states, especially in the Deep South, licence to drive an automobile is given at 15 years of age.

14

neighbours' lawns at $1.25 (10 shillings) a time.[1] This is how he pays for the 'gas' and maintenance, too.

During the evening, at the weekend or for holidays there is always a family car[2] and we found that American housewives complained only about imperfections of the bus service *during the daytime*. Its shortcomings during the evening or at weekends rarely interested them.

English people's grumbles about bus services ranged much wider. In most instances, in their previous neighbourhood the buses used to pass the end of the road every five or ten minutes and this facility was sadly missed when they moved out to their new homes. Many were now faced with a service once every half-hour or less. In the pub and the village shop the newcomers were not backward in criticizing the 'terrible' inadequacy of the bus service, as they viewed it; they frequently got little sympathy from the old residents who appreciated the *improved* frequency consequent on the influx of large numbers of new arrivals.

By contrast with America, a frequent source of complaint from English respondents was that the weekend bus services, 'when we like to go and see Mum', were too expensive to allow them to take the children or that they did not start running until 2.00 p.m. on Sunday; many complained that the buses stopped too early in the evening. On most routes the last bus from the city, which was at 10.15 p.m. on weekdays and Saturdays, left at 9.45 p.m. on Sunday. Several households had had the unfortunate experience of failing to get on the last bus because it was full and having to find the fare for taxis. Many had 'just missed the bus' and had had to wait a half-hour or an hour, according to the local schedule. With a couple of tired children and a cold easterly wind it is no wonder that the memory of these experiences lingered with the families which had to rely, if only at weekends, on the public transport service.

[1] This is the price we were charged once a week by a neighbour's teenager son to cut two patches of grass each 20 feet square with a motorized 'roto-scythe'.

[2] The only exceptions were one male old-age pensioner, one widow and one divorcee.

2

FAMILIES ON THE MOVE

MOST English people hold the view that Americans, in general, are restless and itching always to be on the move: that they change homes more frequently: that they do not approach the purchase of a house with the same sense of permanent occupation as English people do: that the American worker shifts his job with greater frequency and that American firms think nothing of transferring their employees from one side of the U.S.A. to the other. How far are these impressions true? This we cannot answer for the whole United States or the whole of Great Britain, but we can say how far they agree or differ from the experience of the sample of 120 families which we interviewed in each country.

Previous Homes

Table 6 shows that, considered together, American households had made slightly more moves than English households. It is immediately apparent from the table that, as regards the numbers of household removals between marriage until present occupancy, in both countries the occupants of houses on the four lowest-priced subdivisions or estates had shared, on average, a similar pattern of movement; each family had lived in, approximately, two earlier houses or apartments (flats).

But, residents in the two highest-priced groups of houses (E and F) differ markedly from each other in the two countries. American families on the highest-priced subdivision had moved nearly twice as many times as English families occupying similar accommodation. In general, the ages of the heads of these

16

TABLE 6

Average Number of Household Removals since Marriage

Estate or Subdivision	U.S.A.	England
A	2·6	2·0
B	2·0	2·0
C	2·0	2·0
D	2·0	1·6
E	3·0	2·0
F	3·4	1·6
All	2·5	2·0

households tended to be higher (Table 1). The evidence that American families move more frequently is not conclusive.

Present Occupancy

The lengths of occupation of houses on the various estates and subdivisions are set out in Table 7; American families had occupied their present homes some six months longer than the English

TABLE 7

Length of Time Resident in Present House

Estate or Subdivision	U.S.A.	England
A	9 mths.	1 yr. 1 mth.
B	2 yrs. 3 mths.	1 yr. 9 mths.
C	3 yrs.	11 mths.
D	1 yr. 2 mths.	3 yrs.
E	2 yrs. 10 mths.	1 yr. 6 mths.
F	3 yrs. 9 mths.	2 yrs. 2 mths.
All	2 yrs. 3 mths.	1 yr. 9 mths.

families; on average, occupants of the lowest-priced American and of the English council houses tended to have moved in more recently.

Future Moves

Only one-third of all English households gave any indication they expected to move to another house in the foreseeable future compared with one-half of all American households (Table 8). The breakdown of these proportions, given in the table, is interesting. One in five English council tenants hoped to move some time—to get a bigger house, be nearer friends. Most thought in terms of a council house: few expected to buy their houses. By contrast, nearly one-half of the occupants living on the lower-cost American subdivisions looked forward to moving for a variety of reasons, amongst which job transfer and the desire for a larger lot were most frequently instanced.

Their compatriots on the higher-priced American subdivisions were less footloose: only 37 per cent expected to move, the chief reason given being job transfer. Perhaps surprisingly to many English readers, nearly one-half of the English private-enterprise householders expected to move: in an overwhelmingly number of cases the reason given was job transfer. It will be recalled that the English group were some six or seven years younger than the American group with which we are comparing them. Nevertheless, the English figure is still high enough to make one reconsider the notion held by many that young middle-aged Englishmen are stay-at-homes, reluctant to move to jobs in new localities. In fact 36 per cent of these private-enterprise householders had previously been living in distant towns or villages. In every case a transfer of job had been involved and for all but two this had meant a removal of more than 80 miles.[1]

Twelve per cent of all the American families interviewed looked forward to changing homes to get more space around

---

[1] The last residence of 15 newcomers (out of 40) on two English private-enterprise estates included the following: Swansea, Isle of Wight (2), Dursley, Southampton, Portsmouth, Kent, Huntingdon, Forest of Dean, Glasgow, Birmingham (2), Ipswich, London, Canada.

them: in other words, they wanted a larger lot. This was usually coupled with a desire to obtain more privacy, a subject to which we return in a later chapter. Not one English family expressed itself anxious to move to get a larger garden (yard).

Eight per cent of American households gave as their reason for moving that they wanted a larger house. Only 5 per cent of English families gave this as their reason and these were all on council estates, i.e. were occupying the smallest, lowest-cost, houses as tenants: no house-owner wanted to move for this reason.

Table 8 could be misleading. The question asked was 'Have you considered living elsewhere?' Many English respondents replied that they had considered doing so and *if* the husband's job transferred him and *if* . . . etc., they would be prepared to move. It was clear that most were content with their present house and neighbourhood and a removal was not really in the family's plans at that time. The American replies were much more definite. Two out of three occupants of the three low-cost American subdivisions fully intended to move as soon as they could. For example, the outlook of a young couple (husband 25 years and wife 23 years), living on one of the lowest-cost subdivisions, is indicated by this comment on their neighbourhood: 'There are too many children here. Each house is alike. It's a new neighbourhood . . . just a starting place. The neighbourhood will go down. . . . We hope to do better.' This young man was manager of a retail shop with the relatively low salary of $4,500 (£1,607); they had two children. On another subdivision neighbours were described in the following words: 'Generally people are only "stopping over" here.' A third said, 'We knew our stay would be short and we are satisfied.' Invited to explain what was wrong with the house or neighbourhood the wife replied, 'There are too many dogs and too many children'; she had three children under the age of six years herself. 'We need more storage space. We would like a house of better construction.' She regarded her neighbours as of 'low economic level and possessing a limited outlook. I have not been able to discuss literature or politics with any one of them since I have been here.' This college-trained young woman of 28 years was clearly out of her natural environment but she

TABLE 8

Reasons for Expected Future Move
(number of households)

	U.S.A.			England		
	All Sub-divisions	Lower-cost Houses	Higher-cost Houses	All Estates	Council Houses	Private-enterprise Houses
1. Husband's job transferred	13	7	6	18	2	16
2. To be nearer husband's work	3	2	1	1	1	—
3. Desire for more space/larger lot/ more privacy	12	8	4	—	—	—
4. Desire for better neighbourhood	3	2	1	—	—	—
5. Desire to return to old neighbour-hood	2	2	1	—	1	—
6. To be near friends/ relatives	5	4	1	3	1	2
7. Desire for bigger/ better house	8	5	3	5	5	—
8. Desire to own house	—	—	—	4	4	—
9. Other reasons	14	7	7	8	3	5
Households likely to move given as a percentage of the housing group	41	47	37	32	20	44

only voiced, perhaps rather more effectively than others, the outlook of others of her generation and background.

Similar statements were not expressed by English informants. English estates tend to be more homogeneous by class structure. Today the poorest working-class famliies put up with many inconveniences of everyday living in rooms or sub-standard accommodation until they are fortunate enough to secure a council house. The majority find it impossible to save sufficient money for the deposit (down payment) on a private-enterprise house. Having achieved possession of a council house this is the height of their ambition. In England, young professional people adjust their expenditure in the early years of marriage so that they can buy a slightly more expensive house than they can really afford, one which they will not expect to have to leave for ten years or so, even if their economic position improves. To this end they will manage without a motor-car or make do with one which is twenty years old. This the young Americans will not, or perhaps cannot, do because of the social pressures of present-day American way of life. To him a motor-car is both a status symbol and an essential facility enabling him to live a 'normal' life. Both these criteria may become operative in England during the next ten years but, at the moment, many English families believe that satisfactory mobility can be achieved by using public transport; or, alternatively, that the cost of private transport, in the form of a car, is not justified, compared with ownership of a house of their own.

Fortunately for him, the American working-man finds it much less difficult to buy a house: there is little Federal, state- or city-owned residential property for renting. On the lower-cost project the down payment was $400 (£143) plus $285 (£102) closing costs; the monthly repayments, including taxes and insurance, was $89 (£32) on a 30-year F.H.A. (Federal Housing Administration) loan. This outlay included gas central heating, water heater, kitchen waste-disposal unit, kitchen cabinets and fitted cupboards. With four times the weekly wage of the English workman it is clearly less difficult to secure a private-enterprise project home in the United States than a private-enterprise estate house in England.

We have shown that some of the older American families had moved a great number of times: certainly with greater frequency than comparable English families. In part, this was due to job mobility and often change of type of job. Two examples will illustrate this. The first man, a technician, had worked as a building contractor for eight years. Then, for several years he 'sold insurance', i.e. worked as an insurance agent. Becoming dissatisfied with this he trained himself as an instrument technician by a one-year evening course at a local college: he followed this with a correspondence course and, finally, a ten-week course at a government training centre for electronic inspection.

The second man, a professional aircraft engineer, had trained originally as an architect at the Cleveland School of Architecture but, unfortunately, the completion of his course coincided with the depression years of the 'thirties. He failed to secure a post and had to get work in an Ohio State works programme. He was so disillusioned as to his future in architecture that he attended night-school classes at the Ohio State University in mechanical engineering. Subsequently, he got a job with an aircraft firm and during the expansion of the industry during World War II gained advancement. After the war, the firm closed down its aircraft side and he transferred to another firm: he chose one with a headquarters in California, for its climate: here the family lived for two years. Subsequently, with all their earlier friends in the eastern part of the United States he got a transfer back when the firm opened a new plant near Columbus, Ohio. Removals of two thousand miles and more meant little to this family. No comparable cases of people training themselves for completely new jobs were met in our English interviews: the choice of job made on leaving school appears final.

American Mobility

Other factors operate to make the American—particularly the younger generation of adult—feel less permanently established in his new home.

Firstly, the bright young American seems to be able, or thinks he will be able, to gain promotion in his job more rapidly than the young Englishman; as he finds himself able to afford them, assisted if not prompted by his wife, he insists on a bigger house, larger plot, a swimming pool or a place to house the boat which is taken, on a trailer behind one of the family cars, to one or other of the lakes or rivers in the vicinity each summer weekend. These are the symbols and the satisfactions of his success. Similar expressions by a young Englishman would more usually be regarded as ostentatious extravagance and would more likely lead his friends to question his financial wisdom and his common sense.

Secondly, 'Americans are quick to recognize good business', as several put it to us. They know that in the first few years after a new house has been built it usually appreciates in value. Thereafter, even in these days of continuing inflation, the rate of increase in value slows down, even if the actual value does not decline. This is true today in both countries. We found that a number of the older families which had made a practice of moving every two or three years had done so in part to take a profit on the transaction. With their profit they were able to make the down payment on a better house. One American, an artisan living on one of the most expensive subdivisions, had moved seven times in sixteen years; he said that he had 'accumulated sufficient equity', that he had been able to build his present house by direct labour out of the profits of earlier sales. Both he and his wife expressed themselves ready to move again if they found a better house or a better lot. (He was 48 and she 44 years of age.) Another, a garage foreman, also living on one of the higher-priced subdivisions, was largely influenced to buy his present house because it was readily saleable: the type of house in an older suburb which they had been living in immediately prior to this had been becoming less easily disposed of at a good price. 'But we have never bought a home with the idea of remaining indefinitely.' They had moved ten times already, each time within a radius of ten miles of the husband's place of employment which had not changed during the period. Both husband and wife were now 51 years of age.

Thirdly, related to the above, American subdivisions lose 'tone', or change their character, much more quickly than comparable English estates. Perhaps because of the frequent change in ownership, the different material of construction, climate, background of tradition, larger income to spend on alternative satisfactions or for some other reason, an American does not appear to lavish the same kind of care and attention—one could say affection—on the fabric of his house as does an Englishman of similar income and social group. Since most American houses are constructed of wood, any lack of care soon becomes apparent. An American subdivision can look very 'tired' after ten or fifteen years whereas, in the same period, an English estate merely mellows; the brick and stone of the latter do not deteriorate and the gardens (yards) are planted with trees and shrubs which mature to give a more satisfying appearance than

23

it held during the 'pioneer', constructional phase. The process of deterioration on an American suburb is enormously accelerated if one or two coloured families acquire homes on the subdivision. The better-off, more mobile, families sell out as quickly as possible for the best price obtainable, cutting their losses if need be. We met several older families who had solved the problem in this way. Newcomers who replace them are less well-off financially and/or are also coloured: the subdivision 'runs down hill' rapidly.

Fourthly, many American houses are built by contract labour. When an Englishman proudly boasts to his friends that he is 'having a house built' he usually means he has found a builder who is already developing an estate with houses of, at most, three or four basic designs to a set price. Our English friend selects his house, or his site; maybe he specifies certain minor alterations or additions to the design and he will undoubtedly choose the colour of the wall distemper or the kitchen sink. But little else. Only rarely will he employ his own architect or erect a house of an exclusive design since this is recognized to be more expensive. By contrast, in America, except on the lowest-cost 'projects', the American realtor (estate agent) sells the lot and the newcomer erects a house to his own or an architect's design, as we have said already, usually in timber, although an increasing number of houses are being erected with parts of some walls comprising stone facings or 'veneer'. Almost everywhere, the basic framework of the house is wood although the basement will be constructed with cement blocks. The actual construction may be handed to a builder who has contracted to build the whole house. Or the owner may act as his own contractor, getting carpenters to erect the fabric of the house, a firm of flooring specialists to lay the floor covering, a friend to put in the electricity services, while, if he fancies himself as an engineer, he may install the furnace bought as a package deal from the down-town store. This practice of 'do-it-yourself' and of mutual help between friends was met in many households: it is probably based on two aspects of American life which are alien to most of Europe. Firstly, many present-day urban Americans are not more than one generation removed from the farm, where 'do-it-yourself' is an everyday experience born of necessity. Secondly, American professional men, especially the college-trained professionals, have spent some periods of their life performing manual occupations, during vacations and at weekends, in which they acquired useful basic skills in building methods and practice.

A home erected by direct labour in this way may take upwards of three years to build, literally around the family installed in a couple of habitable rooms. Elsewhere, in America, we met several families who were living in the basement, practically below ground, whilst the constructional work of the rest of the house was being carried on above them during the summer evenings and at the weekends. One professional householder and his wife, whom we interviewed, were completing their third house in nine years, each time building bigger, more expensively and in a better neighbourhood, as they 'acquired equity', as they described it, from previous sales. The last was a magnificent home set in one and a half acres[1] of tree-covered slope and included full air-conditioning installed by the husband, apparently ably assisted by the wife. They had, unfortunately, reached the stage where the present home was so large as to be less easily sold at a profit and they were rather worried as to their next move. The husband's age was 38 and the wife's 36: his occupation, instrumentation engineer.

Finally, a factor which seldom operates in England in the mid-1960's; many Americans still look back with nostalgia to their early days on the farm and they cherish an ambition to own a place in the country with a few acres which they can farm, or play at farming, maybe on a part-time or share-cropping basis.[2] When they are first married, of necessity they rent an apartment (flat) in the city or near the university if still 'at school', but each subsequent move takes them farther and farther out to 'open country' living. An example was the

[1] The minimum size of plot on this subdivision was set at one acre by the local council of the county district because it was not served by a main sewerage scheme. For septic tanks this large plot was deemed necessary. This standard of provision would seem unduly extravagant of land to an Englishman.

[2] Subsequently, I met several university professors who were operating farms of from 50 to 100 acres in this way. They employed most of the labour, directing the operation in their spare time. The customary nine-months engagement for university academic staff helped them in this since they could be free from mid-June to mid-September.

young graduate research engineer who had lived first in the city and moved out to his present house (which he built with direct labour—mostly his own) in order to get a large lot; this was also one and a half acres which he considered the minimum for his three children and three dogs. His main aim in life was to buy a farm of 25 acres or so at least 10 miles farther out, but not too far to prevent him keeping on his work as an engineer designer. On this small holding he proposed to raise cattle and, eventually, be his own boss so that 'the harder I work the more I shall get'. He did not make it clear how he was going to live off 25 acres and, clearly, he had some doubts himself because he was not proposing to give up his engineering job immediately. But, he had worked his way through college to get a degree and was confident he could achieve his ambition. Both he and his wife had been born on farms and liked the life although they preferred the salary of the professional engineer. The existing motor roads make it quite practicable to live as far as 25 miles from the city job and it is conceivable that better roads now being built and faster cars may even increase this distance in the future.

This engineering graduate was not unusual. A university agronomist had bought his present lot because it was a large one (one acre) and because it was in the country on the edge of the city. He also had been brought up on a farm and his work was related to farming. His ideal lot was five acres farther out into the country so that his two children (now 6 and 4½ years of age) could keep a pony. This he wanted when he purchased his present lot three years before but on his salary at that time he could not find the requisite down-payment.

In neither country was there much evidence of hankering after the old neighbourhood or old friends. Only seven Americans and four English households wished they lived nearer their old friends or relatives or wanted to return to their old neighbourhood.

Miscellaneous reasons for expected future moves included: English—emigration (3), noisy neighbours (1), wanted a smaller house (1); American—wish to live in a smaller community (3), intend to move on retirement (2).

An important contrast in the way of life of people in the two countries is brought out by Table 9. More than half of all English husbands and wives had spent their lives within 10 miles of where they were now living; one-quarter of the American husbands and wives had been born within 10 miles of their present residence. On the three lowest-cost estates in both countries, twice as many people were born within 10 miles as was the case on the highest-cost estates and subdivisions.

TABLE 9

Places of Birth of Husbands and Wives

Estate or Subdivision	Within 10 miles of Columbus, Ohio, or Bristol, England		Elsewhere in U.S.A. or Great Britain		Outside U.S.A. or Great Britain	
	U.S.A.	England	U.S.A.	England	U.S.A.	England
A B C {Husbands	21	40	39	16	0	2
{Wives	21	45	38	12	0	3
D E F {Husbands	13	25	45	35	1	1
{Wives	16	26	42	32	2	1
All {Husbands	34	65	84	51	1	3
{Wives	37	71	80	44	2	4

Two quotations, answers to the interview question 'Have you considered moving again?', epitomize the attitudes of people in the two countries. An Englishman, after he had recovered from the initial surprise that such a question should be deemed necessary, replied, 'Only if we found a better place. It would have to be good to beat this. . . . Besides we can't afford it.' An American answered for many of his compatriots, 'We knew our stay would be short. We are satisfied.'

3

CHOICE OF NEIGHBOURHOOD

EARLY in the interview, householders were asked the reasons which caused them to choose the neighbourhood in which they were living in preference to other neighbourhoods. Respondents were not prompted in any way. A great variety of answers was received, including the vague 'we just liked the district or the neighbourhood'. Some may have had other reasons for choosing the particular neighbourhood which they failed to advance. For instance, all needed a home—many had been living in un-self-contained or unsatisfactory accommodation and were prepared to seize almost any vacant house within their means. This often became apparent later in the interview. In the United States 13 per cent, and in England 6 per cent, explained their choice of neighbourhood in such words as 'We needed accommodation urgently and this was available'. The majority exercised more discrimination, as we shall see.

In both countries, unfurnished accommodation is difficult to come by and those of our samples who occupied rented homes had had, in fact, little if any choice when selecting them. In England, these were all tenants on council housing estates; in America there were only seven tenants all living on lower-priced project subdivisions. These were not included in the analysis which gave rise to Table 10, i.e. the reasons which lead householders to choose their present accommodation. The American group is too small from which to generalize: the reasons given by the sizeable group of English council tenants are separately summarized in Table 11 and discussed at the end of this chapter.

The categories which appear most important to American

28

TABLE 10

Reasons for Choice of Neighbourhood[1]

England	Per cent
1. Open country near	48
2. Ease of access of husband's work	30
3. Design of the house	22
4. Small deposit (low down-payment)	16
5. Reasonable accessibility to the city	16
6. Town and country planning control	14
7. A vague liking for the area	14
8. House was good value for the money	12
9. A good residential area	10
10. A new house	10

U.S.A.	
1. Ease of access of husband's work	26
2. A good school system	26
3. House was good value for the money	22
4. A vague liking for the area	22
5. Close to shops and services	18
6. Low, or no down-payment	17
7. Close to school	15
8. Design of the house	15
9. Proximity to relatives and friends	14
10. Larger lots available	14
11. Needed a house and this was available	13
12. House was the right size	12
13. Layout of the subdivision	11
14. Reasonably accessible to the city	10

Note: The figures represent the number of persons volunteering each reason expressed as a proportion of the total number of persons in the sample. Some respondents gave several reasons: it follows that the aggregate of these percentages exceeds 100 and would be meaningless for purposes of comparison.

and to English buyers of new (or virtually new) property, judged by the frequency with which they are put forward as influencing their choice, are set out in order in Table 10. Nearly one-half of all English house purchasers chose their new neighbourhood because it had open country nearby. This factor does

[1] Given by 10 per cent or more of persons interviewed in each country.

not appear at all in the United States list: in fact, only six persons gave it as influencing their choice. 'Ease of access to husband's work' appears at or near the top of both lists but in America this distinction is shared with 'a good school system' which does not appear at all in the English list. 'Good value for the money' is number three in the American list and appears as eighth in the English one. The existence of town and country planning controls are considered important by English buyers but this factor scarcely influenced Americans.

The broad similarities, or contrasts, in reasons for selection, set out above and in the table, clearly need closer examination adequately to appreciate the situations in the two countries. In the following paragraphs we shall bring out differences in the way of life—differences in land development, house purchase, personal mobility, availability of services and the like.

Open Country

All English estates were peripheral to the city, all American subdivisions except one had at least one side to the open country. As mentioned above, the most important factor influencing English buyers was the existence of open country nearby, i.e. 48 per cent; another 2 per cent said they wanted to be away from the centre of the city although this does not necessarily mean in a district abutting the countryside. Few Americans considered that proximity to the countryside was a good reason for selecting a new neighbourhood in which to live. Several factors can be advanced to explain the contrast. We have already shown in an earlier chapter that several American families chose their neighbourhood because large lots of one acre or half an acre were available. These could, clearly, only be found near open country but the purchasers made it quite plain that it was the actual lot and not the open country which determined their choice.

The English countryside is often thought of as the townsman's 'play-ground'; rambling clubs use it: motorists and cyclists picnic there or 'potter' ('putter' in the American vernacular) round the country lanes: primrose gatherers, bluebell pickers, hop pickers, for these and for countless groups of townsmen the countryside has an important place in the seasonal pattern of recreational activity and appreciation. A high standard of aesthetic beauty of landscape need not be present: the most important feature of the countryside is often its accessibility which for many, especially for those families without a car, means relatively close proximity: 'We are not in the country and not in the town. We can go for a walk beside the river . . . living here is still like a holiday' was how one housewife, with excitement in her voice, described her new surroundings.

During the last decade, an important, and from our evidence seemingly successful campaign has been waged in Great Britain, by the Ministry of Housing and Local Government, county planning authorities and various specialist voluntary societies, which is designed to make people aware of the imminent danger of losing much of the English countryside if building development were allowed to go unchecked. A couple of years before our interviews an area of land adjoining our private-enterprise development area had been proposed as a 'green belt' by the local planning authority, although it had not then been approved officially by the Ministry of Housing and Local Government. This received considerable publicity in the press and elsewhere and as many as 14 per cent of English householders mentioned planning control ('zoning' in American parlance) as a factor influencing their choice.

The near countryside is rarely regarded by the American as an amenity in this sense. For this kind of appreciation of nature he drives along a series of straight motorways to a city, state or national park where, on Sundays and holidays, in company with thousands of others, he can find shade (and mosquitoes), organized playing space, rigidly controlled parking arrangements, and barbecue cooking facilities (braziers and fire-places) all neatly and efficiently erected about a cooking area; the park store (trading post) will supply provisioning deficiencies; if the area is woodland, 'trails' will be defined and carefully signposted. Written in this way, the American park system may seem to an Englishman a dreadful substitute for the 'real' countryside, but when you have to endure temperatures of 95° F., day after day, accompanied by night temperatures which do not fall below 70° F., even an Englishman flinches at the thought of a walk in the noonday sun. In the heat of a Middle West summer, my wife and I habitually and frequently drove the 15 miles out to the nearest park just to enjoy a walk in the relative cool of a pleasant wood by the longest trail which encircled it in fifty minutes. On other occasions we drove 120 miles each way, along miles and miles of straight four-lane highway, merely to experience a day in what by English standards was only reasonably-pleasant picnic surroundings. The word 'countryside' has aesthetic overtones to the average Englishman, as it has come to have for numerous American visitors to England who return to extol the charm of the English countryside. To describe the American countryside an American uses the words 'farm country' or 'open country', but rarely 'countryside'.

The rate at which the countryside is being swallowed by the outward march of the town was clearly worrying some of our English householders. One, a man of 54 years, had already suffered: 'When we were married twenty years ago we went to live at Fishponds (an adjoining neighbourhood on the townward side of the developing area) to get as near to the country as possible. But the town seems to reach out so fast into the country.' He appeared to have doubts as to the ultimate effectiveness of the green-belt policy. To still fears that they might be engulfed by later developments many occupiers of urban-fringe estates have seized upon the promise of the green-belt policy as a drowning man clutches a straw.

In our interviews in America we tried to find the American reactions to this outward march of city-fringe suburbs. The peripheral estates being built in England at the present time are allotting one-eighth or one-tenth of an acre for a house selling at £2,500 to £3,500 ($7,000 to $9,800). In America, prospective purchasers with comparable jobs are demanding, and getting, at least one-quarter, and frequently one-half, acre lots. As a result open-country land is being used up many times faster. 'Were Americans worried about this?' we asked. With very few exceptions no one was. 'There is plenty more land to be had and it is only farm land anyway', was the sort of reply we received frequently. Several of the more serious-minded persons we met—professors and higher executives—agreed that open land was disappearing too quickly and that it should be controlled in some way: but not the British way—that was 'socialized' planning.[1]

In their replies, the secondary problems created by uncontrolled suburban growth, for example accessibility and increased cost of town services, were brushed aside. New motor roads were being constructed to take care of the accessibility problem and 'Nobody goes down town any more. We use the shopping centres': these last are peripheral to the bigger towns. The effect on public transport services was seen by them to be minimal since 'Nobody walks today'. Yet, the distance of most new subdivisions from the few public transport service routes and from the shopping centres and schools makes it imperative that two out of three families should decide to have a second car for the convenience of mother and children throughout the day when father is away at work.

Size of Plot (Lot)

Many more English families would like to own a half- or one-acre plot if they could afford to do so. Now, the populations of Bristol and Columbus are approximately the same. Land on one of the best American subdivisions had been bought for $150 (£53) per foot frontage, roughly $1,000 (£356) an acre. Building land farther out into the country beyond the English private-enterprise estates, which should, theoretically, be cheaper than that on the estates with which we were concerned, has been sold recently for £4,000 ($11,200) an acre. At this price only the really well-to-do can afford large plots of land. The English house-owners we interviewed had bought both house and land for less than £3,000 ($8,400). The high price of building land and consequently small building plot is, in England, accepted as one of the facts of modern living and only one householder, who had a slightly larger garden (by a few

---

[1] For these people socialized planning meant restrictions on the use of land by the State or Federal government. Some were, however, prepared to accept this restrictive control if exercised as a local 'ordinance' by the local rural or city council.

square yards) than the others, stated that he was influenced by the size of his plot. By contrast, 14 per cent of Americans were influenced by this consideration.

This desire by Americans for large lots derived from a variety of causes. Many house-owners craved privacy (see Chapter 4). One wanted a swimming-pool—in this instance for use and definitely not as a status symbol. Another, a minister who had been born and reared on a farm, had bought five acres but subsequently sold off four as building plots. He explained that he had wanted space for his teenage son to pursue various 4-H farming projects in which he was interested at that time. A third family had searched for three or four years to find a sizeable lot, not too far from the husband's work in the city, which would offer some unusual feature, as long as it was being sold at a price they could afford. Finally, they succeeded with a lot which afforded a variety of slope, several trees and a 'ravine' as they described the deep-cut stream at the bottom of the garden.

The attitudes of English and American households concerning the proximity of the countryside can be summarized as follows: in both countries there was an urge to move farther out from the town—to get near the open country. In America: 'We like to live out. We don't want houses back to back and side to side,' said one: his wife interjected, 'Out. But not too far out.' Closer living is accepted as inevitable in England. Most English housewives (homemakers) would echo the sentiments of the American homemaker, perhaps for different reasons, and amongst these there would loom large the availability of a convenient bus service.

Husband's Journey to Work

Ease of reaching the husband's place of work was the most frequently mentioned reason given by American householders for the choice of neighbourhood: 26 per cent gave this as one of their reasons for choice. The same factor came second with English householders, although the proportion (30 per cent) was actually higher: this proportion held true for the lowest-cost and the highest-cost estates. However, the residents of the three lowest-cost American subdivisions rated ease of getting to work much more highly: one-half of all the families gave this as a factor.

But ease of access meant two entirely different things in the two countries. In America, it was the ease with which the husband (and sometimes the wife as well) could get to work by private car. Thus, the proximity of the subdivision to a fast motor-road driving towards the centre of the city was of prime importance. This will no doubt be equally important in England in the future when a system of motor-ways has been built and the proportion of car-owners to the total population has increased. In England, fewer cars have meant that most housewives are marooned in the home all day. The farther out from the city centre they live, the fewer buses there are. This has increased the pressure on land near the city periphery. In addition, because of the greater density of population and relative scarcity of building land, land values are much higher than in most areas of the United States.

In general, in England, accessibility of workplace meant, for the breadwinner as for his wife, the availability of convenient public transport services. Indeed, the infrequency and cost of fares by the public bus system was a general complaint of the majority of council-house tenants, many of whom had been living near the central areas of the city and had not had time to adjust themselves to the inconvenience of longer journeys to work. Their relatively low wage levels would clearly prevent the majority from buying their own mobility for many years. Amongst council-house families 36 per cent owned and had a car or motor-cycle to take them to work; 12 per cent used public transport and 42 per cent walked or used a push bike. The position on the private-enterprise estates was easier: here 62 per cent used a car or motor-cycle, 18 per cent used bus or train and 8 per cent walked or used a pedal bicycle.

The largest single employer of labour in the north Bristol fringe, where all the survey areas were situated, was an aircraft firm at which 24 per cent of all house-owners and 12·9 per cent of all council tenants were employed. The factory lies in an entirely separate, peripheral suburb and by public transport a journey into the centre of the city and out again to the factory was necessary. Many workers formed car pools (although often

35

only one car was used by four users), others hired a bus to take upwards of thirty men to and from work.[1]

Had they been able to find comparable accommodation nearer to their workplace many of these workers would undoubtedly have taken it, but little new housing development was taking place nearer to the factory at the time. The position has not changed greatly since because of the stranglehold on new development exerted by the 'green-belt' and the tight control of new development maintained by the county planning authority.[2] This control has been necessary in order to keep urban sprawl in check but, because of the largely uncontrolled pre-war and war-time industrial location and expansion, planning control has made it increasingly difficult for newcomers to the city, and young people setting up house for the first time, to find homes within reasonable distance from the factory, remembering that for English workers 'reasonable' in most cases means reasonably easy by public transport. The location factor which seems most important to a working-man without a car was summarized by one, who described his new neighbourhood as 'not too far to go to work. The handiest place to find a decent house.'

Accessibility of City Services

A smaller number, 16 per cent in England and 10 per cent in America, looked for 'reasonable accessibility of the city centre': in both it was mainly the households with higher incomes who demanded this facility: 'We like the country but we also like to be near a big city which provides the services we need occasionally': this was from a young English professional.

In England, good bus services direct to the city were for many residents on private-enterprise estates one of the main advan-

[1] One of these privately-hired buses took 47 workpeople from the council estate daily: it left at 6.40 a.m. and returned to the estate by 6.30 p.m. at a cost per head of twelve shillings (i.e. $1.68) for five days' travelling. This is one of the few examples where English people had showed initiative and set up their own organization to satisfy an evident local need.

[2] For American readers it should be explained that an English county covers an area many times larger by population and in extent, than the American county. The area and total population of Gloucestershire, in which our estates occur, are 800 acres and half a million persons, respectively.

tages of location even where there was a family car. On council estates where buses were less frequent, and not always direct to the city centre, this was one of the chief grumbles: 'It's no pleasure to go to Bristol because it's so tiring to take the children. . . . The children get bored at weekends. They want me to take them somewhere but I can't afford the fares'; this housewife had young children and all her relatives lived in Bristol. 'I go (to Bristol) when the children are in school. I start out early in the morning as I have to be back at three', i.e. when the infants' school closes for the day.

Whilst bus services are still demanded by, and are especially necessary for, the less well-to-do, in England, they have declined in importance in America, and the following comments which illustrate this fact typify conditions as we found them on peripheral subdivisions there: 'I haven't been down town (i.e. to the business centre of the city) since we have lived here.' 'I haven't used a bus for five years,' said a young housewife, 23 years of age with two young children; they owned a seven-year-old Ford but the husband had the use of his firm's truck which he brought home each evening. These were both working-class householders. 'I don't go on a bus if I don't have to,' remarked the 34-year-old woman school-teacher. She and her husband shared a two-year-old Ford and twelve-year-old Chevrolet; this is typical of the transport equipment for young families when the wife has a job, as it is for older middle-class families with incomes of, say, eight to ten thousand dollars a year upwards (£2,850–3,570).

When we were living in Columbus, Ohio, many of the higher-priced, new subdivisions, which were being opened up at that time, were within a stone's throw of one of the two new motor roads with restricted access which had been driven straight through the countryside towards the heart of the city. The description of one of our subdivisions, 'This is excellent trans-portationwise', held true for many others so situated. The future development and distribution of the population in Great Britain will, no doubt, be similarly influenced as the national pro-gramme of motor roads proceeds. As we write, a storm is raging on one of the English estates, with which we are concerned, because a new proposed Ministry of Transport road will, in the opinion of the local residents, pass too near the houses. In America, this facility would most likely raise the value of the houses and the desirability of the neighbourhood as a place to live in. English householders can only see the destruction of the open countryside and hear the noise of cars and lorries (trucks) rumbling by. They fear that their properties will fall in value because of this.

Whether English people will continue to use the new city centre shops, which are reaching to the sky in many of our English regional cities, once every family has a car, is not as clear to me as to the business men financing their development. In the United States, traffic congestion has reached the point where you only use the city centre if you have to and then preferably after business hours: 'I never use down town (the city centre) except for telephone shopping'; this remark of one American housewife is being echoed by an increasing number in that country as more and more residential subdivisions and new shopping centre 'plazas' are being built on the city fringes. Many workers who have to journey to the centre of the city each day are leaving their cars at the bus stop on the fringe, in order to avoid the expense of a day's parking charge of a dollar (7*s.*) or a dollar-fifty (10*s.* 6*d.*); in the largest cities it may be as much as two dollars (14*s.*). We found that a number of wives drove their husbands to the bus-stop each morning and met them there each evening.

Closeness to shops and everyday services was rated fairly highly by a proportion of American housewives; 18 per cent listed this as a factor in their choice of home but two-thirds of these lived on two of the lowest-cost subdivisions. Half as many, only 8 per cent, English housewives living in private-enterprise houses considered this important enough to influence their choice. The two proportions are not strictly comparable however. Proximity for the American housewife meant a district shopping centre within easy reach, say *twenty minutes' drive* to a peripheral shopping centre, where around a single parking lot a whole week's shopping can be done in an hour or so, including making occasional purchases of clothing, or furniture, taking a couple of her husband's suits to be cleaned or having her hair trimmed and set. For the English housewife, convenient

38

shops meant a butcher, baker, grocer and hardware store within *ten minutes' walking* distance of her home. On sizeable English private-enterprise estates this is usually an automatic provision and the shops in our survey areas were opened almost at the same time as the houses were occupied. On one council-house estate the building of the neighbourhood group of shops was delayed and the housewives interviewed were bitter in their condemnation of the local authority for neglecting a facility so necessary for them to be able to live a satisfactory (English) way of life.

Generalizing, it can be said that the occupants of the low-cost dwellings, in both countries, laid greater emphasis on the proximity of shops and services than did those in the higher-priced dwellings who had greater mobility given by more cars and fewer small children.

A Good School System

A good school system ranked equal top in the list of reasons for choice of American neighbourhood. It was not mentioned by English householders. Children on the three lowest-cost American subdivisions attended schools under the Columbus school authority. Those on the three higher-priced subdivisions attended those run by the Worthington Incorporated District (i.e. a 'fringe' urban district council) which was well known to provide better-than-usual school facilities; needless to say the school taxes were correspondingly higher. The figure of 26 per cent, as representing those residents who chose their neighbourhood partly because it operated a good school system, would, in fact, be doubled, to 52 per cent, if it were related only to those three subdivisions. This gives a fairer measure of the importance placed on this facility by the residents living in an area known to have a good school system.

How far this choice reflected the *educational* aspirations of the parents and how far it revealed *social* desires is difficult to judge. At least one, a maintenance engineer, admitted that he was influenced by the 'type of people . . . educated people. It gives the children better friends.' For the majority, the educational clearly far outweighed the social advantages. Many spoke of the high cost of the education tax but no one grumbled about it: they were well aware of this before they moved to the neighbourhood.

On the opposite side of the city of Columbus was another incorporated district with an equally good name for its school system. Here property values and taxes were slightly higher, but two of our residents said that they had rejected this neighbourhood because there was too great an emphasis given to social status, although they had been attracted by the high educational standard provided by the local school system. 'We didn't want Arlington because of the great amount of status seeking and we could not give the children what the others in Arlington get,' said a professional engineer. One is tempted to comment that this parent really felt that he could not afford or could not justify the cost of the social provisions of the Arlington schools. This would be unfair and probably untrue; the observation was echoed by others on the subdivisions where we interviewed: it was also made to us by parents we met when attending social functions elsewhere, particularly those arranged in association with the Ohio State University. One householder, who was a university professor, stated that he bought a house in his present neighbourhood because not only was there a good school system but 'the children come from all economic levels, not like Arlington'.

Linked with the alleged superiority of the local school system was the physical proximity of the school and the fact that many children were able to walk to it: 'The school system is good and the children can reach it (the school) without special transport. There are other places in Columbus as good and cheaper but they haven't the convenience of good schools.' This particular subdivision was tucked away in the angle between two main roads but adjoined the school property: 'The children do not have to cross a traffic road,' said another.

On the low-cost American subdivisions the proximity of the school to the home was mentioned by several residents but no reference was made to the quality of the school system.

The English educational system is a national one and standards do not vary greatly from locality to locality although certain schools gain better reputations than others. The social

backgrounds of children attending different schools vary according to the general make-up of the neighbourhood. No comment
concerning this fact was passed by parents on English private-
enterprise estates. However, it was a source of satisfaction for
several council-house tenants that the neighbourhood was
peopled by 'respectable' people but who were not 'snobbish'.
'I would avoid an area where people were better off because
the children would mix with other children (who were better
off) and get discontented. Here we have similar-sized families
and similar incomes,' said one. His wife was influenced with
the converse: 'I should hate to live near families where they use
bad language or the husband drank,' said she. These quotations
lead naturally to our next section.

A Good Residential Neighbourhood

In both countries a significant number of house-owners were
influenced by the fact that they were buying in 'a good residential neighbourhood'. For some, this meant little more than
that the houses were attractively arranged. But 'This area is
strictly residential' from an American implies a recognition of
the value of the zoning controls exercised by the council of the
local incorporated district (town council) in which the subdivision was situated. As we have already indicated, other
Americans we met would not accept that English-style town
and country planning was either desirable or necessary for them
as a general principle. Yet, the ones with whom we spoke admitted
that some residential neighbourhoods were good mainly because
there was control on the type of development. This reason
entered into the choice of 35 per cent on one of the better subdivisions. As one observed, in explaining why he rejected other
parts of the city fringe, 'There are no good residential areas in
the east (of the town) except Bexley, and that will grow older
and older. . . . In the east there are no zoning ordinances.'[1]
Another said, 'The land beyond us is zoned for residential
development by the Worthington City Council.' This is not
town and country planning. Or is it?

English house-owners came out bluntly with 'We were

[1] In English, 'planning regulations'.

41

assured that no council houses would be built in the area', or 'It's residential, we shan't get any factories here'. It is recognized by everybody that both these kinds of development tend to depress the price of good-class residential property. The English Labour government of the late 'forties tried to mix property of all types and price in close proximity but it did not work: the majority of English house-owners unashamedly invoke planning regulations when it suits them to keep lower-priced or council development at a distance. American house-owners seemed slightly uncomfortable about their zoning regulations which tend to segregate property of different price levels; it does not seem to accord too well with the 'all men are equal' concept.

The expression 'good residential neighbourhood' holds status or 'snob' overtones in both countries. For instance, it was clear to us that a successful American sales manager had chosen his new home mainly because several senior executives of his firm also lived there: he played golf with them on Saturday morning. Unfortunately, there were indications that he was suffering some disillusionment: throughout the interview, he continually referred back to the extra cost of taxes, interest on capital etc. consequent on living in the 'good residential neighbourhood'. Yet it was clear that he would never have openly admitted the real reason why he chose his house and neighbourhood.

In both countries, the 'tone' of a neighbourhood mostly increases with the dimensions of the plots, which, usually, in turn, increase with the value of the houses built on them. But for a number of reasons, of which price is only one, the size of the American lot increases more rapidly with house price. In America, the low-cost project house will stand on a plot of at least 50 ft. by 150 ft.: this is larger than the average English council house plot of, say, 30 ft. by 80 ft. So much plot area is occupied by a single-storey house that it is not surprising that the typical English house, because of the higher price of building land, is a two-storey building, and is frequently semi-detached (a 'double' in American usage) or one of a terrace of four or more. Because American lots are larger their houses can be larger and are mostly single-storey bungalows, one-floor-plan houses as they are described.

Design and Layout

In Britain the days are past, and in America are passing, when developers can get away with crowding a plot with too many houses, built in straight rows, along streets which intersect at right angles: we now demand variety in layout as well as in house design. Layout or lot design in some form was recognized as important by 11 per cent of American purchasers when choosing their home. This is a significant proportion but it should be noticed that it occurs well down the list of reasons for choice of neighbourhood. Thus, from one of the more-expensive American subdivisions came the comment, 'We liked the open aspect of the subdivision and all the trees.' From one of the low-cost subdivisions, which was austere enough by modern standards, one of the more thoughtful homemakers (housewives) said, 'I like the court (cul-de-sac) layout.' Her opposite number on an English council estate was of the same mind: 'We had the choice of two (houses) here. I chose this cul-de-sac . . . there's more safety for the children.' Groping for words, one fairly inarticulate English householder felt that his neighbourhood was 'more countryfied. It is not crossed by main roads.' The absence of traffic was appreciated especially by young mothers but, also, the road serving a cul-de-sac is usually narrow and, since there is one outlet only, the residents tend to meet each other more often. An English housewife living in a corner house of one of these cul-de-sacs said, 'I see and speak to people as they pass.' The husband, thinking of the other side of his property which abutted a semi-main road, interjected, 'We live on a wide road and do not get to know the people on the opposite side': he was less keen to do so. Opposite preoccupations are revealed by the two sexes here.

There was, however, little evidence that English residents, owners or council tenants, were greatly influenced by the layout of the neighbourhood *before* they moved into their property, although several became aware of advantages and disadvantages *afterwards*. In fact, council tenants had little choice and only one private-enterprise occupier seemed to have given the subject serious thought. Another had made his selection virtually by rejection: a great deal of 'infilling', i.e. building on small

parcels of vacant land, has taken place in urban fringe neighbourhoods to British towns and cities since World War II. These
locations had been rejected by this prospective buyer because
'All the new houses are mixed up with dirty old houses', and
he added, 'on an estate you are all starting together. We thought
people would be more friendly and it has worked out that way.'
The attraction of a brand new house clearly influenced a great
many householders but since they did not specifically refer to
a new *neighbourhood* we were unable to accept this as evidence
for an awareness of the importance of design and layout of the
neighbourhood.

As regards the design of the house, on two American subdivisions most (85 per cent) of the occupiers interviewed had
first bought their lots, and then arranged with an architect for
a house to be erected to their own design. The remaining 15 per
cent were either second occupants or had bought from a small
speculative builder. No two houses were exactly alike. For the
larger group the design of the house could not be a factor in
the choice of neighbourhood, and excluding these people the
analysis would raise the proportion for category 8 (Table 10,
U.S.A.) from 15 to 22 per cent—a relatively high order of
choice: it refers mainly to lower-priced project houses.

Design of the house came third in the list of reasons for choice
of English neighbourhood (22 per cent), i.e. the same proportion
as American project house-owners.

Americans visiting Britain find English housing estates monotonous—semi-detached, three rooms up and one or two down,
in brick or rough-cast (stuccoed) finish. The sameness of this
style of building they compared unfavourably, and rightly so,
with the variety of their own styles—one-floor-plan, one-and-
half storey, split level, ranch style and Cape Cod. Their houses,
which they always refer to as 'homes', are mainly of wood, and
can be painted a great many colours, although white is most
commonly met because it reflects the summer heat; as we have
seen, stone, brick, tile and plastic shingle facings are being increasingly used to increase the variety, reduce the cost or bother
of maintenance and for status reasons or simply because, at the
moment, it is fashionable. With wood the main building medium
for the structure of the house, variety of style is more easily

achieved. Whilst this was the special feature of the individually-developed subdivisions we found the low-cost American project houses more monotonous and dreary even than the early council estates built in England forty years ago.

Since World War II, most developers in England have tried to introduce a little more variety of design into their estates, and this includes councils. In the survey neighbourhoods streets were not always straight: there were some cul-de-sacs: bungalows and semi-detached houses occurred on the same development: both traditional and chalet-type designs were employed. Nevertheless, by American standards the average English estate is still stiff, too uniform and monotonous. But there have been improvements which in our neighbourhoods had clearly found favour with the house-owners we interviewed: 'We chose the house rather than the neighbourhood,' said one, and this was true of others. Many were bungalows (one-floor-plan houses). Ten per cent said that they wanted a *new* house by which they no doubt implied new design as much as new materials. This quality was scarcely mentioned by Americans: probably it was taken for granted.

Accommodation

Twelve per cent of American, but no English, householders stated that they chose their house because it was the right size, i.e. had the right number of bedrooms, a basement or the right-sized lounge or sitting-room. English interviewees were no doubt influenced by the fact that the usual English house has at least three bedrooms, basements are almost never supplied and the ground floor area beneath three bedrooms gives enough room for either two smaller or one large sitting-room. A trend has become noticeable, during the last year or so, however, to build more two-roomed bungalows and chalet-type houses, where some of the bedrooms are built in the roof, and the total floor space is less than in a comparable three-bedroom house.

'We needed more accommodation' was the usual reason given when the size of the house was referred to. With the younger English families this usually meant that they had been living in rooms and now had children (arrived or expected); younger

45

American families had bought a cheap housing-project, two-bedroomed, one-floor-plan house in place of the apartment they had rented previously. Few could afford to buy a larger home even though they would have liked more accommodation: several spoke of future plans to furnish a guest room or a recreation room in the next house they bought.

One, and only one, householder out of 240 had moved into his present house to get *less* accommodation: 'The house we lived in was so large—it was two storey—and I was at work. This is easier to take care of.' This American homemaker (house-wife) worked as an inventory clerk at $200 (£71) a month. The husband was a press operator in an engineering works earning $400 (£142) a month. They had two children at school, a boy of 16 years and a girl of 11 years.

Good Value for Money

With the keen business sense the world has come to expect of them, nearly one-quarter of all Americans (22 per cent) selected their house and neighbourhood in part because it represented good value for money; 'We got this for less money', or 'The houses were awfully nice for the price'. Only half as many, i.e. 12 per cent, English house-owners said that value for money was important in their choice. Relative scarcity of new houses, no doubt, influenced them in this undiscriminating attitude. But also there is possibly a greater tendency in England to leave it to the expert, in most cases the surveyor of the building society, to decide whether the property is good value for money. In England, maximum advances are, normally, only obtainable if the property is newly erected and soundly constructed.

The number of house-owners who stated they were attracted by the low deposit (down payment) expressed as a percentage of all owners was 16 and 17 per cent for England and America, respectively. The American figure must be adjusted, however, since on the two highest-priced subdivisions most of the houses were 'custom built' for their occupants and there was no question of a low deposit. Expressing the figure as a proportion of the remaining 73 houses we get 26 per cent.

On an American housing project only five per cent of the

purchase price might be required as down-payment. On some, U.S. Service 'veterans' were able to obtain 100 per cent advances through the Federal Housing Administration (F.H.A.) or the Veterans' Administration.

In England, 90 per cent is normally advanced by building societies for new houses on building estates. For individually-built new houses advances would not normally be greater than 80 per cent and are frequently less.

In general, American house mortgages on individually-built properties are obtained by a bank advance or from a building and loan association and the purchaser is expected to find at least one-third of the purchase price. For most young married couples this is impossible and they begin married life in an apartment house and then move to a project development. We met one young American house-owner who was determined not to do so. Having bought the lot he wanted, he said he had 'shopped around for two years' before he found a bank ready to lend him a sufficiently large proportion of the cost to enable him to start building. He was exceptional. Others were working their way up from housing project to better housing project to custom-built homes on their own lot.

The younger people, especially in America, stressed the attraction of the low down-payment. A thirty-year-old insurance underwriter, with two children, earning about $5,500 (£1,964) a year, said he was 'desperate for a place and this was the lowest down-payment of any available'; the family had been living in rented rooms. The second, a thirty-year-old technician, earning a similar salary, and also with two young children, had been living for three years in rooms with his parents: 'We had no money and a low down-payment was essential.'

Both these people bought homes on a 'project' where deposits of 20 per cent were accepted, the houses had cost $12,000 (£4,285) to $13,500 (£4,821) so that the deposit was of the order of $2,500 (£890). On the cheapest project where interviews were taken the deposit was $685 (£245). The cheapest of our English private-enterprise houses were £2,000 ($5,600) each on which a 10 per cent deposit would amount to £200 ($560): a similar deposit but met from, perhaps, one-quarter the income; it is easy to see why many lower-paid English workers

47

wait for a council house. Those who make the grade and find the deposit do so with difficulty or luck—for instance if the parent of one of the partners comes to their aid. An ex-council house tenant who had become a house-owner explained: 'We looked forward a long time until we could save up the deposit for a house.' It was his first house: he was now 37 years of age and had four children.

The English house-owners we met had, however, passed this first hurdle and were more concerned with the size of their regular repayments. These last formed roughly similar proportions of the households' incomes in both countries: in England the average annual rate of repayment worked out at £125 ($350): in America at $900 (£320).

Finally, a note on resale values. The continued rise in postwar residential property values in both countries has induced an attitude amongst house-buyers that future disposal at a profit is automatic, an attitude which contrasts markedly with the experience of those of us who remember conditions in the early 'thirties. Only 4 per cent in each country stated that they had bought their homes with a view to their being easily re-saleable. 'It is all new property here and therefore there is little chance of the property depreciating in value': this comment came from a 34-year-old, English, commercial traveller (salesman), who had been transferred by his firm and expected another move in due course: he was the exception probably because he expected to have to realize on his property soon. He was confident that selling at a profit would present little difficulty. Recent increases in property values in England have proved him right.

Friends and Relatives

For American house-buyers a fairly important factor in the choice of neighbourhood was its situation relative to the homes of their friends and relatives: 14 per cent instanced this compared with only 8 per cent of English families. But a more marked contrast exists in the responses of the working and the middle classes. In America, the occupants of the lowest-cost properties, i.e. working-class or very young professional families, scarcely ever referred to proximity to relatives and/or friends. In

England, the reverse held true; the working-class, council-house tenants, in choosing their neighbourhoods (if they had a choice at all), were very concerned about where relatives and friends lived; 28 per cent gave this as a factor influencing their decision. Admittedly, many house-owners had come from another town, and a much higher proportion possessed a car or motor cycle, but there is, clearly, a difference of outlook between the two groups. The better educated, better paid, professional classes in England appear to be more independent of the ties of family and old friends than their opposite numbers in America or of the working class in England.

Friends and workmates play an important part in helping a newcomer to select his new home and neighbourhood especially when a change of town is involved, for at such a time the new-comer is ignorant of the local situation and needs advice on location, the integrity of the builder and so on. Also, he has all too little time to spend on exploring when his family is, perhaps, still living in another town. The young man who was moving to Bristol from London, England, ' . . . dashed down from London on a couple of day trips and the Downend houses were available. I liked the houses and we bought. I didn't spend much time looking.' He did not see anything unusual or risky in his method of selection: 'We wanted somewhere to live.' An American was more fortunate. He learned of the develop-ment, where he eventually bought his new home, from friends in his home town of Cincinnati, 120 miles away. Quite a number in both countries were introduced to their new neighbourhoods by their workmates who had already bought, or had contracted to buy, houses in the neighbourhood. This had an important secondary effect on their lives in that in both countries car pools for journeys to work, and amongst the wives to take the children to school if need be, were arranged, especially amongst the better off. This in turn led to family friendships.

A Friendly Community

The main reasons for choosing the new neighbourhoods have been referred to already but a few other interesting reasons were given by both English and American residents. For instance, six of the 60 families who lived in the incorporated district of Worthington, Ohio, stated that they were influenced by the 'small-town character' of the older part of this settlement which had been founded a long time ago by American standards, i.e. in the early nineteenth century by New England settlers venturing into little-known Ohio. New England associations were referred to with respect: 'Worthington is a New England-type village. There is a small-town atmosphere and people are very friendly.' A second used almost the same words and added, 'It's slow moving and neighbourly.' A third said, 'We prefer a small town. I don't like enormous schools. We are both from a small town.'

It is conceivable that these three statements are expressions of satisfactions subsequently achieved *after* taking up residence. All three were earnest, thoughtful men, and it is possible that they genuinely took this into account before purchasing. We cannot be sure. However, Worthington prides itself on its historical origins and traditions which it keeps alive with festivals, through articles and frequent references in its own newspaper and utterances in the churches and the council chamber. Several of its churches are at least a hundred years old: a great age by Middle-West standards. The 'city' council includes many well-educated professional people and is seen to pursue an enlightened policy. Finally, and perhaps most important, all three of these informants, like many others of their neighbours, were 'small-town' men themselves; they had been brought up in or near country towns, and although they were compelled by the nature of their employment to live near a big city, they appreciated the 'small-town' environment, which made it possible for them to take part in civic affairs, i.e. to elect people they knew and met in the street or at church, to assist in running, and feel proud of, the fine local school, to attend neighbourhood celebrations of many kinds, to be able to shout when they disagreed with something—and have notice taken of their clamour.

The English private-enterprise houses were built in an area which was the responsibility of a local authority which did not enjoy this kind of prestige. It was a village grown too rapidly into a suburb. When subsequently, the newcomers failed to secure the services and attention they felt was their due from the district council they expressed their dissatisfaction vociferously with results which are indicated later (Chapter 4).

A Vague Liking for the Neighbourhood

People are often much more conservative in their likes and dislikes than they imagine. Nearly a quarter (22 per cent) of all Americans said they chose their new neighbourhood partly because they like the 'north end' or the 'west end' of the city, which ever was appropriate. Fourteen per cent of English house-owners behaved similarly. From America: 'We always liked the "north end". 'We prefer the "north end".' 'We have always lived in the "north end".' 'We like the "north end". We're used to it.' From England came similar expressions of vague liking: 'Even when we were courting we said we should like to live at Downend.' Few of these people stopped to analyse why they preferred the district in which they sought their new home. They just liked the area because they had been familiar with it for some time and if this suited them they saw no need to put themselves out to seek similar or other advantages somewhere else.

Besides this conservativeness, there were other factors determining the choice of a familiar area. A newly-developing area close at hand is more easily brought to the notice of prospective occupants by advertisements and, equally important, is more easily visited. Eight per cent American, and 7 per cent English, owners bought their houses, partly because they either knew the developer, or the builder, or the property was especially recommended to them by a friend. One man, an American: 'I used to work for the builder and I had faith in him.' From another, 'The developers are local people, not somebody moving in from New York and then moving out. There's never the same house in any one block.' Personal or semi-personal recommendations like these were clearly important determinants in the final choice of these people.

The sector of the *city* in which a resident used to reside was in most instances chosen originally with a view to accessibility, especially of work place. A subdivision or estate in the same general direction is likely partly to fulfil similar requirements. An example of what can be termed impulsive buying yet which, at the same time, secured work-place accessibility was supplied by an English owner-occupier who had been a tenant in a council house: 'We had intended buying,' he said, 'but, for no reason at all, right out of the blue I saw an advert in the local paper of a house for sale at Downend. So I just came out here.' He could give no other reason. It was in fact a neighbourhood with which he was familiar and it did not make his journey to work more difficult. *The long-term result of this choice of a more-or-less familiar neighbourhood tends to cause a town to grow, in the future, still more in the direction in which it has grown in the past.* This is a common factor of English town development, and was especially so before 1939, i.e. before town and country planning took a hand in the ultimate shape of towns. I have not seen this 'law' enunciated anywhere, however.

SPECIAL NOTE

Council House Tenants having Choice of Neighbourhood

Thirty-nine council house tenants were given a choice of estate: for eight of these the alternative was a very large housing estate on the opposite city boundary which for various reasons had gained a less-pleasing reputation. As one put it, 'We had no choice except B . . .' Another, a little more circumspect, said, 'It was this or B . . . and we had heard unpleasant things about B . . . . Warmley is a better district.'

Linked with most of these dislikes, however, were the obvious advantages of the estate selected and more than half, 54 per cent (Table 11), chose as they did because it was easier for the breadwinner to get to work. Many would have endorsed the opinion of one of their number: 'My husband's work comes first. We want to live near his work.' In this particular instance the work-place was now 'round the corner' instead of an hour and a quarter's journey away by bus.

More than a quarter were influenced in their choice by the proximity to, or accessibility of, friends and relatives. At some time during the interview, the majority of the remainder regretted that parents or friends were so far away.

The most-distant council estate, at Yate, was more than ten miles from Bristol and a journey home to 'mum' could take more than an hour by bus, and if made often could be unduly expensive, for a household with young children. All the tenants on this estate knew of these difficulties before they accepted the offer of a council house: many others rejected the offer of a council house at Yate for this reason. But for some the need to obtain *any* accommodation was deemed to outweigh the disadvantage of location. Some young housewives found it more difficult than others to make the mental adjustment involved in the physical separation from family and friends.

TABLE I I

Reasons for Choice of Neighbourhood
Given by Council Tenants
(England)

	per cent
Ease of access of husband's work-place	54
Close to friends and relatives	28
Good or better residential neighbourhood	18
Open country near/away from centre of city	13

For most of the council-house residents, 'This is the best estate of the lot' summed up their appreciation of their new neighbourhood, *after* they had had experience of living there. Only 18 per cent said they arrived at this conclusion *before* they made their choice: most of these were influenced by the appearance and layout: few were able to make themselves clear as to what they meant by a good neighbourhood. As with those who bought their homes, many factors influenced their choice: few found words to explain them as succinctly as the following housewife, a young woman of 26 years of age, who had been a Post Office telephonist: 'We asked for this estate. It's nearer my husband's work. There's not much traffic. We are used to this end of the town. It's quiet . . . many places are noisy because of aircraft. It's a small estate.'

A small minority recognized the advantages of living near the country and away from the town: 'We were offered Yate, Keynsham and Warmley but we chose Warmley because of the openness.' The 'openness' here referred partly to the open lay-out of the estate but more especially to the 'openness of the countryside' around: on the estate itself houses were fairly tightly packed consistent with what is considered good planning for council estates. One or two had reservations about such near-country living: 'My husband was not very keen to go to Yate at first. He was doubtful about a country district but I was very keen to get my own home.' This couple had been living in rooms with her mother. The husband soon found a friend in the neighbourhood, with whom he walked up to the pub occasionally, and the family settled down happily.

Most of the tenants echoed the comment of the young motor mechanic who was earning a little over £9 ($25) a week, i.e. 'We were ready to take any house offered because we were fed up with two rooms'. 'We were only too pleased to get in. The other place was terrible. It's a wonderful place this'; this older couple (both 47 years of age), the husband a general labourer earning £8 ($22) a week, had been moved from a cottage, which had been condemned by the sanitary authority, where they had lived for 13 years. A young couple said, 'My wife was expecting and we were given a week's notice. We had to go. Our unfurnished flat was ever so damp and we had wood worm. . . . We were afraid for our new furniture.' Another family had had to leave their old home because it was to be demolished under a road widening scheme.

Only one in five, i.e. 19 per cent, of the council-house families had previously occupied a whole house to themselves. Many could say with the young washing-machine mechanic, 'We had a bedsitting room and shared the kitchen, bathroom and toilet, but we fell out with the family we rented from.' For them, as for all tenants on these peripheral council estates, the weekly expenses soared when they moved to their new house, but 'This is a palace compared to our other place', and 'We were so excited. I don't mind where we live as long as we're happy.'

4

NEIGHBOURHOOD APPRAISAL
AFTER OCCUPATION

IN general, the assessments of their neighbourhoods given by English and American householders *after* they had taken up residence show close agreement (Table 12): 83 per cent of American and 87 per cent of English residents assessed their neighbourhood as either 'Good' or 'Excellent': 17 per cent and 13 per cent respectively described it as 'Fair' or 'Poor'. These proportions were distributed fairly evenly over the different English neighbourhoods. All but one family amongst the 40 on the two more expensive American subdivisions described them as 'Good' or 'Excellent'.

TABLE 12

Neighbourhood Appraisal After Occupation
(as per cent of total)

	U.S.A.	England
Excellent or Good	83	87
Fair or Poor	17	13

Satisfaction

The satisfaction mentioned most frequently by English residents, i.e. by more than 20 per cent, was, firstly, the joy of living in or near to country surroundings, secondly, the pleasure resulting from having such good neighbours and friendly people around them and, thirdly, the satisfaction derived from seeing their children so happy, healthy and contented (Table 13). Of these three categories, only the friendliness of the people was mentioned by as many as 20 per cent of American householders; the other more important features for them were the proximity of schools, and the ease with which facilities, mainly shops, could be reached.

TABLE 13

Satisfactions Derived from Living in the New Neighbourhood
(as per cent of total)

	U.S.A.	England
Country surroundings	8	42
Cooler/fresher air	4	12
Quiet	0	18
Clean	0	14
Close to school	28	3
Good for the children	18	27
The friendliness of the people	25	26
Easy access to city	0	12
Nearness of facilities: shops, etc.	24	13

Country Location

The feelings concerning the near-country location held by families prior to moving to the new location were, in the main, carried over and are reflected in their expressions of satisfaction with the neighbourhood. Relatively few Americans, actually only 8 per cent, said they derived satisfaction from the near-country location, and eight out of ten of these lived on one subdivision where the lots averaged half an acre or more; they liked the view, the birds, etc. By contrast, 42 per cent of all English families mentioned country surroundings in some form or another. 'It's open out here. I don't think I could be shut in again,' said one husband. His wife, who was in complete accord, added, 'I've woken up since I've been out here.' And another: 'I can't explain really (why I like the neighbourhood). For one thing, it's quiet . . . on Sunday it's dead and that's how we like it.' A further 12 per cent enjoyed the cooler fresher air compared with only 4 per cent of American householders who mentioned these qualities. Fourteen per cent of English, but no American, replies included reference to the cleanness and healthiness of the neighbourhood. This was felt to have been beneficial for the family, especially the children. Furthermore, it made housework easier; for instance, housewives (homemakers) now found it necessary to wash the curtains (draperies) much less often. 'It's all so clean and fresh' was typical of many of these comments.

The country surroundings no doubt meant for some English families, as for most American, larger gardens (yards) and more spacious layout. But most English people were clearly looking farther afield. 'I like the open fields': this sentence was often used in English interviews but never in an American. 'We can go for walks on Sunday without having to use buses,' came from a young, as yet childless, couple. Two council tenants, clearly, held similar sentiments: 'There are new walks for the children. It's more healthy'; and 'We go out for walks with the children in the summer. All of us are more healthy.' The last family had lived the previous ten years in the wife's parents' home in an old worn-out neighbourhood, where 'The toilet was up the top of the garden (yard) and we had one tap in the house—downstairs'. So often the appreciation of country surroundings was linked with the welfare of the children.

Friendliness

In each country, about a quarter expressed themselves especially pleased with the general friendliness and neighbourliness they had met with from their new neighbours. In America 25 per cent and in England 26 per cent (Table 13) expressed this view in a great variety of ways. From England came the comments: 'People are nice to know. Most families seem to be young': 'People are more friendly here than at H. . . .' From America: 'We've got wonderful neighbours', and 'The best (neighbourhood) we have ever lived in. Not one family is hard to get along with.'

Many families linked this general friendliness with the fact that neighbours were 'pioneering' together, as one American husband put it. 'It's a new neighbourhood and women automatically get together,' said another. But do they? Are all new neighbourhoods equally friendly places to live in? Do all, or most, newcomers rate friendliness as so important? Examination of the replies, neighbourhood by neighbourhood, brings a negative to all three questions. Only on two American subdivisions (the highest-priced) and one English estate (intermediate) did as many as 50 per cent of all householders instance neighbourhood friendliness as one of the main reasons for liking their new locality. Fourteen per cent of the total American replies stated that they liked the neighbourhood because of the 'small-town' community activity which they had shared since arrival: this presumably includes friendliness of the local people.

By contrast, on one English (private-enterprise) estate only 2 per cent, and on three American (intermediate) subdivisions only 1 per cent, mentioned neighbourhood friendliness in this context. Yet, on the lowest-priced American subdivision, incidentally the one most recently built, 35 per cent, well above the average, had found their neighbourhood a friendly place to live in, and thought to say so when asked what they specially liked about the neighbourhood.

Occasionally the establishment of friendly relations was ascribed, incorrectly as we have seen, to the superior or special social status of the community. An English house-owner gave it as his opinion that 'The people are nearly all middle class. We like the people': and from a council tenant, 'The rents are higher here than at other council estates and only those who can afford it move here': this was true. A one-time tenant of a council house, now an owner-occupier, was a little more specific, although he had to grope for words to express himself: 'Compared with a council-house estate, to us we look at it in a more favourable light than some others, perhaps. On a council estate there are a few rough families. Here you don't get them. This is a good place to bring children up in.' This quotation leads to the next, frequently expressed, satisfaction.

58

Good for Children

Parental decision as to whether a neighbourhood is good for the children, or not, seemed largely to depend upon answers to the following questions. Are the children healthier? Have they good playmates? Is the school readily accessible? Are they safe when at play, or going to school, or on errands? In other words, are they reasonably protected from traffic dangers? Having answered these questions to their satisfaction, 27 per cent of all English, and 18 per cent of all American, families gave as their reason for liking the neighbourhood that it was good for the children.

The high value placed on proximity of the school, especially in America, has been referred to already. 'It is possible for the children to walk to school without crossing a busy highway' was the typical reply which drew attention to the traffic hazard for children. Nevertheless, in both countries, the safety of their children was a major source of worry for parents. 'We like the narrow roads and the cul-de-sac. It slows the traffic down. They're wonderful things these cul-de-sacs': this came from an English housewife. If only town planners and architects would move amongst the people who have to live in the streets they design we might have more cul-de-sacs, fewer accidents and many more contented mothers.

The safety of the children seemed to come to mind more frequently with American than with English parents. Thus, a mother who lived on a low-cost housing project, which she disliked intensely—'A housing project? Never again!'—nevertheless admitted that the neighbourhood was 'wonderful for the children. The parents watch their children. We have a supervised swimming pool.' Another, a near-neighbour, commented that the children of the neighbourhood were all clean and that they got along well together.

English parents seemed more concerned about the influence of the neighbourhood on their youngsters' health. 'It's nice for the child. It's very healthy. It's off the main road and quite safe (to play). She (the daughter) was like she was penned in before.' Or, 'The children like it. There's more freedom for them.' Both of these replies were from council tenants who, like many others of their neighbours, mostly poorly-paid artisan families, had

59

been living in two rooms in tiny, out-of-date houses in mean, narrow streets, where the only nearby play-place for small children had been the pavement and the gutter, places which were unhealthy and dangerous. The comment, 'The garden (yard) is long enough for the child to play in', expressed a mother's deep satisfaction that her child was able to play in safety on a piece of grass under the parent's watchful eye, probably for the first time in her life. One local authority tried to educate its new tenants to a more open layout of garden and separated the front gardens from the pavement (sidewalk) by a very low wall and *no gates*. This open-plan garden layout with no walls or hedges, the norm for new American housing developments, was rejected vociferously by all the newcomers as being unsafe for the small children who could run straight out into the street. Eventually the council had to give way and erect gates.

Nearness of Facilities

In most cases, 'close to facilities' meant being close to shops, although some Americans included church, school and 'small-town' services, such as dry-cleaning and hair-dressing. More American than English families found special satisfaction from being near to these everyday facilities, i.e. 24 per cent, compared with only 13 per cent for English families. As we have already explained the availability of facilities meant easy reach by car for Americans; whereas for English families it meant within easy walking distance, say, a quarter of an hour. In England, the private-enterprise estates included groups of neighbourhood shops, grocer, butcher, hardware, etc. The provision of shops was only referred to by residents of these neighbourhoods where, because of the situation of the home, two or more neighbourhood groups of shops could be reached relatively easily. Thus, 'We have five different lots of shops within reach'; or 'Local shopping is well arranged with a few shops here and a few shops there'. The absence of shops on the council estates caused a great deal of dissatisfaction and this is referred to in some detail in a later chapter.

Accessibility of the City

No American families gave as their reason for liking their new neighbourhood that it was within easy reach of the town: 12 per cent of all English families did so. This reflects the fundamental difference in the way of life of the two people. Many more English, than American, families had been born and had spent *all* their earlier lives in town and some, clearly, felt the break with familiar surroundings when they moved into their new homes. For those who had no car—especially the women—this meant being severed from their families and friends for weeks or months at a time, even though the distances involved were not great—seven to ten miles. To reach friends and relatives in most parts of the city involved a bus journey into the city centre. Not so for American housewives most of whom had the use of a car some days each week: they could travel from door to door to visit friends in other parts of the city usually without going through—in fact, usually avoiding—the city centre.

In America, special shopping, for example, clothes and furniture, are obtained 'all over', as we were frequently told by Americans, i.e. at various peripheral shopping centres or often in nearby towns. Some of these housewives, especially the ones with young families, made the journey to the city centre not more than once a year. In England, by contrast, almost all special shopping is still done in the central shopping areas of big cities and towns. 'We are close enough to the country but not too far to be able to go to the city. I would not want to go out farther', were sentiments which the majority of English residents on peripheral estates would echo.

Maintenance of Property

The 'tone' of a neighbourhood is very largely indicated by the care taken to keep property in good repair, tend gardens, etc. For reasons given earlier, English estates tend to retain a fairly uniform, reasonably high level of outward appearance for many years—i.e. for 20 to 30 years, at least, and some very much longer. Nevertheless, some English families found living on a new estate novel enough to express their satisfaction as follows:

'Everyone is buying a house. They look after the property and surroundings and they lift the tone up. They don't want anybody to do something for them.' This came from a house-owner who had lived on a local authority estate where the council retained responsibility for outside maintenance, i.e. carried out the external painting and repairs, trimmed the front hedges and the like. Clearly, he was proud to be able to look after the property which *belonged* to him. Another family, a young couple, 24 and 23 years of age, in their first home, had come from a rather poor neighbourhood. They were delighted to find that 'nobody hangs the washing out in the front garden (yard). Everybody looks after their gardens.' For good measure, the husband added, 'I can't think of anything I dislike', to which the wife added, 'No! Nothing!' A third house-owner, again one who had lived in a council house, replied in the same vein, 'There's not a line of dirty washing to be seen. It's all beautifully white.'

American references to maintenance of property were more numerous but were directed mainly at the upkeep of the house and the lot: 'They are new houses, properly kept up.' 'The houses are well kept up with flowers and shrubs to improve them.' No references were made to washing hanging on the line, presumably because a great deal of American washing never sees the light of day but is washed, spun dry and hung in the basement to finish off.

A minority of Americans, mostly those in the more expensive houses on larger lots, liked the neighbourhood because of the attention which people gave to their yards (gardens). As one husband said, 'We are both gardeners', but he said it in such a way as to draw attention to the fact that he was conscious that, as Americans, he and his wife were unusual. When your garden is laid low every winter with severe frost and the roses are frequently 'frozen clear down to the ground', as we were told, you have to be keen on gardening to indulge in it seriously. Another husband, who clearly had less time for the pastime, nevertheless gained a great deal of pleasure, and a little tolerant amusement, from watching his wife's efforts. 'My wife likes to play about with flowers.' He, like most American husbands, was content to keep the grass cut down to six inches with the motorised roto-scythe (lawn mower), which is the necessary standard equipment in most American homes where the lot is a quarter of an acre or more, most of it given over to grass.

General Satisfaction

An attempt has been made in the foregoing lines to indentify the feelings of satisfaction which the great majority of new-comers found in their surroundings. For most, 'It all adds up' would be the best (American) description of their feelings. For Englishmen: 'Pleasant surroundings, pleasant people, nice houses.' Or, 'I just feel quite at home. I settled in very quickly': a hint of surprise and also achievement is apparent here. These were two English housewives, living on private-enterprise estates, i.e. families who chose their new homes and neighbourhoods themselves.

What of the council occupants who were *allocated* houses? Most families, husband and wife, were very happy in their new surroundings, but in one home we found disagreement. The husband was describing the estate as 'It's lovely here', when his wife cut in with 'No! It's not!' It appeared that, after eighteen months, she still missed the shops, the friends and her old associations. Nothing was right about the neighbourhood, except the house itself, and that she said she could never bring herself to leave. Something seemed to be missing and, eventually, the husband supplied a clue: 'If she could only bring her mother here she'd be all right.' This woman was exceptional in that she appeared quite incapable of adjusting herself.

Many other council housewives (homemakers) entered their new life with similar doubts which fortunately they resolved very quickly: 'I wouldn't have chosen Yate. Now I wouldn't go back.' 'Now we've come out here we wouldn't want to go back to Bristol or anywhere else.' These comments were from people whose '. . . only reason for moving was to get a place of our own. It was heaven. Even for £2 8s. 0d. (in this case, a quarter of the man's take-home pay) a week it's heaven': these unsolicited testimonials should repay all the effort which was expended by councillors, and others, to house wage-earners whose income was too low to enable them to buy a house of their own however urgently they needed one. They should also provide food for thought for zealous city councillors who insist that people who lose their homes through redevelopment and similar programmes should be rehoused in the same neighbourhood, in blocks of flats if need be. We would repeat that, eventually, most families learnt to like their new neighbourhood and to appreciate that a new home on a new estate outweighed the disadvantage of being up-rooted from familiar surroundings. But it takes a little time to adjust yourself when you are dropped down miles from home with a couple of youngsters under 5 years of age, and no money, no time and little energy to slip home to see 'mum'.

Dissatisfaction

The chief causes of complaints about the neighbourhoods in which the newcomers found themselves are set out in Table 14. They differ markedly with the country. In America, they fell into two groups: a quarter were looking forward to the time when they could afford better accommodation in a better neighbourhood; 11 per cent criticized the layout of the subdivision.

TABLE 14

Reasons for Disliking the New Neighbourhood
(as per cent of total)

	U.S.A.	England
Layout of subdivision or estate	11	13
Lack of entertainment facilities	0	4
Bus services, infrequent, expensive, too far away, interference from	3	8
Wanted to move to a *better* location, lot, house	27	2
Children's play space, safety recreation facilities needed	3	1·2
Services inadequate, shops	0	17
Local authority provision (including schools and library)	2	10

In England, dislikes were spread over a wider range, the most frequent being inadequate shopping provision, especially on council estates, shortcomings in connection with layout of the estate, too few places for children to play in safety, and assertions that the local council had failed to provide adequate services.

Amongst American families, the most important reason for disliking the present neighbourhood related to the house and its immediate surroundings: 27 per cent put this forward. Of this group, a half were looking forward, with confidence, to the time when they would live in a better-class neighbourhood. As might be expected, these were all living in the low-cost houses. 'We want to move out of a housing project. The people are not of our kind.' In fact, at the time they were interviewed this family could well have afforded to live in a better neighbourhood, although when they moved in, three years previously, they may well not have been able to do so.

In general, English house-owners appeared quite content with the house and garden they had purchased and the status of the neighbourhood in which they lived. Some were ready to move if their financial situation improved considerably or if the husband's place of work were changed, but it was clear that they would be content with their present accommodation for an indefinite period. But desire to move at the moment! 'No! No! No!' replied one proud and happy housewife.

Among the 120 English families, only two had definitely decided to move—because they wanted a better house or garden, or both: they were both council-house tenants.

'When the children are ten we should like to move to a nicer neighbourhood for them.' This observation, which was made apropos of the playmates they expected to find there, came, not from one of the 'class conscious English', as the Americans often speak of them, but from an American mother living in one of the medium-priced houses. Many references were made to the large number of children in the English neighbourhoods but none to their social equality or inequality. It is true that comments were passed on variations in the standards of behaviour of different families but none proposed to move on this account.

English mothers wanted 'a nice park for the children', and 12 per cent stated that the provision of facilities for children's safety or for their recreation (the two were often linked) were inadequate; these facilities English parents expected the local authority to provide automatically. None indicated that they felt it was in any way their responsibility to initiate anything in this regard.

A major source of annoyance on the English estates was the tardiness shown by the local education authority in providing, what the parents regarded as absolutely vital, a school, or schools, round the corner for children of all age-groups. Seldom was allowance made for the usual, and often necessary, time-lag involved in the creation of a need (in this case, the building by private enterprise of a large number of new houses), the recognition of that need by the local authority, preparation of plans, their submission to the Ministry of Education, and approval of the financial expenditure by the county council. Only two American householders complained that the school was too far away: both were living on low-cost subdivisions. It will be recalled that the existence of a good school system was one of the main reasons for choice of homes on the three highest-cost subdivisions, and complaints from them on this score were not to be expected.

Shopping

Perhaps the most noticeable contrast in attitudes in the two countries, observable from Table 14, was that 17 per cent of English, contrasted with zero Americans, complained about inadequate shopping facilities. In England, all the grumbling came from council and none at all from private-enterprise estates. The latter were fairly well provided with shops from the outset, and as one resident said, 'We only need to go to Bristol for clothes and Christmas shopping. We don't need the cinema —we've got television.' The dependence of the English housewife on her little group of local shops is illustrated by the comment of another of these private-enterprise residents. Her husband had replied to our question as to any dislikes he held with regard to the neighbourhood by an emphatic 'I have no dislikes', when she added, 'No, because there is a shopping centre quite near', as if there was nothing else to be said. By contrast,

66

on a council estate a husband who had replied, 'It's lovely here', was corrected by his wife who exclaimed, 'No! There are no shops!' Several spoke of missing the launderette (laundromat), which they had used regularly in their previous neighbourhood. (It was probably the sociability which they missed as much as the convenience.) Americans do not expect to find and, in general, do not want shops to be located on a residential sub-division. In fact, there would be an outcry against such development. Similarly, Americans *expect* to find it necessary to use the car to change their library books or, indeed, to buy postage stamps since the English type sub-post-office in every neigh-bourhood is not met in the United States. It once took the author a half an hour to walk, in the sweltering heat of a Middle West mid-summer day, to the nearest post-office to which he had been directed with the words, 'It's five minutes along North High.' It was—five minutes by car.

Planning and Layout

The category with which both English and Americans were most in accord was that the layout of the estate or subdivision left something to be desired. These complaints emanated mainly from the cheaper areas where houses tended to be huddled closer together. In each country, over 10 per cent felt that 'someone' 'somewhere' could have done 'something' which would have achieved a better layout. In England the 'someone' was usually assumed to be the local district council which they felt sure held the responsibility under town and country plan-ning legislation. In fact, it is the county council which holds ultimate responsibility. In America, complainants were less specific and there was only a vague feeling of frustration that someone ought to have intervened at some point in the develop-ment. But in both countries the burden of the complaint was the same: 'The houses are too close.' An American felt that this 'squashes individuality. I want more peace of mind.' An English husband tried to express the same idea when he said, 'If you stand near the window, everybody can see what you're doing', to which his wife added, 'It's awful!' The closeness of the houses to each other led to secondary complaints of lack of privacy, noise from the neighbours, children running over the gardens, etc.

Too-close proximity of the houses constituted the main complaint of Americans, but the English householders were more demanding, because of their different needs or customary provisions and, maybe, their greater education in, and familiarity with, planning precept if not practice. They asserted their rights for the provision of a children's recreation space, and an imaginative arrangement of shopping facilities. One informant was particularly scathing, although perhaps less well-informed, about the population necessary to support a full-scale shopping centre. He spoke as follows: 'The estate is not well-planned. There is no park for the children—it's important. The houses are too stereotyped. It's pre-war building thrown together by builders and their friends on the council. They could have shown more imagination of arrangement. The estate has been designed by a clerk of works and not an architect. This has been built as an extension of Bristol—as a suburb—but it could have been considered as a satellite. They could have collected the shops together as a shopping area instead of in little groups.'

In America, because land is cheaper and because of the way in which development takes place, the better-off householders obtained a better layout and were able to appreciate more readily the ultimate physical pattern of their neighbourhood. On comparable estates in England, the early purchasers, although all had seen plans of the proposed development, frequently had no clear conception of what the estate would look like when completed, or else had a wrong one and consequently suffered disappointment: 'I wouldn't like to buy off the plan again. I should like to see it (the houses) erected. We thought it was going to be "Good" but now it is only "Fair" . . . because of the bus route and the road-house.' 'If I could afford it I would move but it's too much an upheaval and too expensive. If we lived off this main road we wouldn't want to move.' This owner could have added that the value of his property had been depressed, or at least had been pegged down, whilst his neighbours in other streets a little farther from the bus route had risen. This unfortunate man, and there were dozens of others similarly affected, had bought his house, as he thought, on a quiet side road. But, when a sufficient number of houses had been erected, the neighbourhood petititioned for better bus services and, with the support of the local council, a bus route was extended which passed through the estate past this man's front door. To add insult to injury a licence was granted for a fairly large public house on a nearby vacant piece of land, and to 'improve' the amenities, a hall large enough for public dances was erected and licensed. Unfortunately, for the locality, a great number of people from off the estate used both the pub and dance hall. They parked their cars in great numbers along the streets and some visitors created a noise late at night. This kind of development could not have happened on any of the six subdivisions we examined in America because 'residential' means exactly what it says, residential housing. Nevertheless, Americans can be unfortunate, occasionally, as the following quotation from an interview with one householder demonstrates: 'Just two streets away a good neighbourhood begins. They let a cement plant use the road for a business way.' Because, in England, people still expect to walk to obtain neighbourhood services and amenities, the word 'residential' can include buildings for 'service' activities. When these are installed, usually after the houses have been erected, some residents are liable to be unfortunate, and even those not immediately affected are not pleased. For instance a resident several streets away observed that 'The new pub is not in keeping with the district. I like a pub but not this kind of pub.' He wanted a cosy 'local' pub of the type which is rapidly passing from the English rural scene.

Experience on this particular estate underlines the need for education of the public, on the one hand, so that individuals can make sure of what they are getting, and of local authorities, on the other, so that they can recognize kinds of development which are likely to be unpopular and generally considered undesirable by the residents. Without a fair amount of study of theory and practice, the purchaser of a new 'estate' house cannot be expected to make an accurate assessment of the ultimate pattern of development from an architect's drawings. 'It's very difficult when you choose a place from a plan and it is all fields at the time.' 'When we bought, on the plans a church and a school were shown but no pub. Now, a pub has been built but

69

not the church or the school.' 'We expected the trees to be left and the hawthorn hedge. We expected the council to have done something about it.'

Property development companies building large blocks of flats (apartments) or offices insist that the architect provides a scale model of the development proposed. These models are relatively inexpensive and all residential estate developers might be 'persuaded' to do likewise.

You will notice, in the last quotation, that the resident 'expected the council to do something'. This contrast in the attitudes of people in the two countries towards their local councils showed itself repeatedly. In America, the prevailing, cynical, conception appears to be that you should never expect the local council to pursue a policy which will benefit you, the individual: that the council is mainly concerned with, and controlled by, business and professional men who are in public life for the good of themselves and their friends. In England, the local council is expected to work for the common good of individuals but it is also generally believed and frequently alleged that councillors are too inefficient or lazy, or both, to do so effectively.

The immediate results of the kind of dissatisfactions described above are quite different in the two countries. In America, householders immediately affected by the disadvantageous development would have sold out as soon as practicable to the highest bidders and gone elsewhere before their property had time to fall in value. In England, the disappointed newcomers petitioned the council, at first individually and later organized in an association. Unfortunately, it was too late to right the immediate wrong but later development has been considered more carefully. In this area, as elsewhere in Great Britain, stronger links need to be forged between authority, on the one hand, and the local resident on the other. Channels for two-way communication are especially necessary, and usually lacking, in a newly-developing neighbourhood.

In England, the poorest members of the community, i.e. the council tenants, are, if anything, better protected in the matter of general layout of estates: these are planned as a whole by experienced architects and planners so that as one council tenant was able to say, 'You know it's a council estate but it doesn't look like one.' Admittedly, the houses on council estates are close together—too close by some standards—but provision *is* made for adequate playing fields, school, library and shops, although some of these are often rather tardy in arriving.

Retrospective Thoughts on Choosing a Neighbourhood

Towards the end of the interview every household was asked the question, 'If you were free to choose again which neighbourhood would you choose?' Almost three-quarters of all American and more than two-thirds of all English answered, 'The same neighbourhood again' (Table 15).

TABLE 15

Retrospective Thoughts on Choosing a Neighbourhood
(as per cent of total)

	U.S.A.	England
If choosing neighbourhood now would select:		
the same	73	68
another	27	32
Where another neighbourhood would be selected, would choose (as per cent of number making this different choice):		
a nearby estate or subdivision	75	79
distant town	25	21

The replies varied with the estate: on the two most expensive American neighbourhoods occupiers were more satisfied with their choice than those on the low-cost ones. On one of the latter as many as one half would have made a different choice; the same was true of one of the English council estates where 55 per cent would have preferred another council estate. These two high proportions were occasioned partly by the relatively little freedom of choice in the first case determined by low incomes, in the case of both nationals, and aggravated for English householders by the restricted choice of neighbourhood given by councils to prospective tenants.

Amongst families indicating that they would choose a different neighbourhood, 75 per cent of American and 79 per cent of English householders would have chosen a neighbourhood within easy reach of the town although this might be the other side of town. The remaining 20 or 25 per cent would like to have lived farther afield. For some it was clearly wishful thinking, for example three Americans mentioned Florida, and two Englishmen wanted to get nearer Torquay or the south-western coast. For the others, however, it appeared a genuine desire to live farther away in a small town or the open country.

Absence of a Sense of Community

Finally, in both countries, the absence of any community spirit was remarked on. Yet newcomers are often lonely and would be eager to join local activities if asked. In Worthington, Ohio, where three of the higher-cost estates were located, community activity was well organized and as we have already noted the newcomers were strong in their praise of the 'small-town' atmosphere as they described it. Some residents of other American subdivisions where community activity was lacking drew attention to the great friendliness of other, smaller town, districts. 'People are friendlier at Mount Vernon', a small town 40 miles away. But because of their higher incomes and greater mobility, which the family car offered, Americans were never lonely; they could secure their social satisfaction in other places with relatively little discomfort—bowling, dances, eating, fishing and shooting as well as attendance at church and secular gatherings.

British families with less money to spend on social amusements and fewer family cars still think, and often act, parochially. 'Somebody' ought to set up a community centre. There's not much team or community spirit yet. There are too few social activities. 'We need more recreation for the young ones. There's no cinema and no dance hall.' 'It's too quiet. My daughter (16 years) doesn't like it. She misses the films, dances and her friends are all in town'; this council housewife (homemaker) got little backing from her husband who cut in with, 'It doesn't make any difference to me. I don't like films and all that. I just have an evening out occasionally.' The place he did not specify,

72

but it was probably the pub. His wife's assessment of the neighbourhood was 'Poor' although she loved her new council house.

The social activities associated with American churches provide opportunities for regular church-goers amongst the newcomers to meet and get to know one another even where other avenues do not exist. From our experience in America, the middle class, but relatively few of the working class, avail themselves of church facilities (see Chapter 10). In England, churches only rarely provided a variety of social activities and a much smaller proportion of the total population attends church regularly. When asked what other services would improve the neighbourhood, only one English resident stated that a church was needed, although one has subsequently been built in the neighbourhood and is flourishing.

For these and other reasons newcomers to a new English neighbourhood tend to remain individuals apart from others in the new neighbourhood for a much longer period than do American newcomers. It makes still more urgent and important the provision of new community buildings, church or secular, and a greater awareness on the part of existing organizations of the needs of newcomers.

5

NEIGHBOURING

A QUARTER of all householders interviewed, both English and American, gave as one of the reasons for their satisfaction with their new neighbourhood the friendliness of the people (Table 13). Analysing the interview reports it was found that somewhere or another during the interview 66 per cent of all American families and 26 per cent of all English families mentioned the general friendliness of their neighbours as being important to them. It was quite clear, however, that friendliness meant different things to different individuals, on different estates (subdivisions), with different income groups: in fact, it varied noticeably with the background of the individual. But, the common denominator of friendliness in neighbours, on both sides of the Atlantic, appeared as '. . . being easy to talk with', '. . . speaks to you in the yard' (garden), both American; or '. . . speaks to you all the time. Has no moods', English. This need for *conversation* with neighbours was mentioned in England by 9 per cent, and in America by 8 per cent, of all householders, proportions which did not vary noticeably from one subdivision or estate to another. The neatest and most telling expression of this need came from a housewife on one of the high-cost American subdivisions who described a good neighbour as one who was '. . . friendly, happy to see you'. Men seemed less bothered about this but the thought was clearly in the mind of the English husband who said, 'They never let you pass without passing the time of day.' But nobody wanted the 'real gabby type' as an American housewife described the neighbour who did not know when to stop talking.

74

What do they talk about? Two American women gave interesting answers to this question, which, incidentally, was not asked by the interviewer. The first explained, 'You are out in the yard (garden) and you see someone working and you say, "Isn't it a lovely day?" and pretty soon you are saying "Isn't your boy in my son's class?" or "Has the boy delivered your papers yet?" and the first thing you know you have found things in common. . . . You just like people, that's all.' The second said, 'Most of us gossip in a friendly way. For example, we say, "Oh! That's the dress you bought at such-and-such a store. Somebody was telling me about that." That's the innocent kind of gossiping.' This homemaker (housewife) recognized the existence of another kind of gossiping but she was far too friendly a person herself to do more than hint at it. Others were less inhibited as we shall see later.

The early offer of friendliness is extremely important to the new arrival. 'If it was not for the neighbours here, I would go back to Frenchay,' i.e. to the neighbourhood from whence she had come, said an English housewife (homemaker).

An English husband was not so sure about neighbours gossiping. He disliked seeing three or four women 'with aprons on talking and gossiping in the street while the children are making a noise and enjoying themselves'. His wife's rejoinder was brief and to the point: 'You're a man!' The wife saw only the friendliness she shared with her neighbours. This was a new council housing estate and subsequent questions showed that the sight of women talking in the street conjured up for the husband a picture of life in the near-slum which he had left behind him. Already, he was jealous of the fair appearance and good name of the new neighbourhood, with which he sought to identify himself.

Linked with the appreciation of conversational friendliness was the feeling that it was an advantage if you shared a common interest with your neighbours; some 8 per cent of American families mentioned this. Most of these were from intermediate-priced subdivisions where the people were younger. In general, common interests were not looked for in neighbours by those who lived on estates or subdivisions which were occupied, predominantly, by people drawn from the lowest or from the highest income bracket. In England, only 3 per cent mentioned sharing common interest with neighbours, as a reason for liking the neighbourhood, and these referred to the experience which most shared, that of bringing up children. Help with the children, however, was mentioned by many more parents in other contexts.

Help in an Emergency

One quarter in the United States, and 70 per cent in England, looked for *help* from their neighbour in some shape or form: help which varied noticeably with the income bracket and the composition of the household. In general, it was 'help in an emergency'. One or two carried it farther: for example, 'A person who would help you in trouble or who would recognize that you were in trouble.' The young mother usually thought of help with the children in sickness. An English housewife (home-maker) added, expressively, 'You *need* help with the children.' Aged 33 years, she had four children whose ages ranged from 3 to 10 years. She did not instance examples but had clearly found her neighbours helpful in this direction.

At the lowest level, help with children comprised advice as to simple childish ailments, but much evidence was given of help, sometimes continued over long periods, which must have involved the neighbours in a very considerable amount of effort and, sometimes money. Two English examples illustrate this. In the first, when the mother was severely ill in hospital, the husband lost only the first two days from work because house-wives (homemakers) on each side came in and assumed responsibility for the two children, both under five years of age. The second, a husband, speaking of the time when his wife was ill, said, 'Our neighbour gave up her job for a week to nurse the wife.' Similar neighbourly actions were met in America: 'Last winter when I was ill my two neighbours came in and took my children (6 and 3 years old), one each, to their homes. My husband was out of town and they prepared food for me.' Quite clearly the severe illness of the mother is one of the most difficult problems to deal with if you have a young family.

The second problem which seems to bring neighbours together in mutual self-help is bereavement or serious illness of a near relative especially one who lives a fair distance away. For one American homemaker, the most important act of neighbourliness had been provided by a near neighbour who, at a moment's notice, took her son into her own home (she already had two small children of her own) to allow her to journey to Georgia, a thousand miles away, to be with her dying father; because of her own husband's irregular hours some form of temporary adoption was necessary. A neighbour round the corner whom we interviewed was equally grateful, but less articulate, about the help she had received from neighbours when she lost her baby. All she could repeat, over and over again, with tears in her eyes, was, 'They're fabulous, I'll say! They're fabulous!' Similar sentiments were expressed by the English housewife whose husband had very recently gone off with another woman and left her with two children. Of her neighbours she said, 'I have found out what a good neighbour is, these last two weeks, since my husband left me.' Neighbourly help in this instance included lending money, for the poor woman was left with no income, until the county welfare department came on the scene; this was a council estate where incomes rarely exceeded £10 ($28) or £12 ($34) a week and the real meaning of the neighbour's help may be imagined.

On the whole, however, the lending of money to neighbours was an obligation which English council householders seemed rather afraid of, and partly explained why some did not want to get too friendly with their neighbours. It was usually linked as follows with the definition of a good neighbour: 'One who keeps herself to herself and doesn't borrow.' Another put it rather bluntly as, 'A lot try to be good neighbours but are on the scrounge all the time.' This kind of remark came only from council houses and never from house-owners in England and never in America. This is not to say that other forms of borrowing between neighbours do not take place; in fact, many seemed to welcome the opportunity to show their friendliness by lending tools, especially gardening tools: it did not worry anybody sufficiently to put it forward as an adverse criticism of their neighbours.

The apprehension of council tenants that neighbours might

77

wish to borrow money may be due to the fact that they were living much nearer the subsistence line than other families we interviewed, and that their recent house removal, with its attendant expenses, had sharpened their awareness of the dangers of neighbours wishing to borrow money from them. In areas of close living, from which many had just moved, borrowing money 'to finish the week out' had been an accepted practice amongst neighbours who had known each other for long periods. These new neighbours were unknown or, at least, untried and, therefore, one had to be careful.

'Settling in' provides opportunities for the display of neighbourly spirit. On one council estate in England several families moved into their new home in the middle of a very cold spell of weather and 'When we came out here first, people were running round helping one another with buckets of coal'. This emergency clearly broke down even an Englishman's reserve. The traditional way to show your neighbourliness in America at times like these is to bring across a pie for the newcomers on their day of arrival. This experience was enjoyed by several families met, but perhaps the finest example of neighbourliness was given us by a stonemason who had moved into a new neighbourhood where three-quarters or more of the residents were from the professional classes. While building his house he injured his back and had to spend several weeks in hospital. When he was able to get about again he still had to wear a brace support and was unable to 'grade' the garden. This expression, for English readers, means clearing up the rubbish and levelling the lot (plot) so that it could be seeded with grass and subsequently cut with the minimum of effort with a wide-cut motor mower—an essential in the hot humid summer, especially when your lot measures an acre, as in this case. This man watched with envy as his neighbours laid out their yards (gardens) and he needed little imagination to visualize the 'jungle' he would have by June: this was early April. But, one Saturday morning at 8 a.m., without previous warning, a knock came to his front door and 'There was all my neighbours, nine or ten of them, and they done all my landscaping for me. They brought tractors, wheelbarrows and rakes. . . . They worked hard from 8.30 to 5.0 o'clock without a stop. . . . They sowed the grass and planted the plants. It gave us a nice feeling.' This last was clearly an understatement.

A wistful comment from a rather lonely housewife makes a suitable tailpiece to this section: 'It's nice to be thought of even if you don't need help.'

Preserving Privacy

My greatest surprise, as an Englishman, came from the limitations which so many Americans put to the desirable activities of a good neighbour, and the stress laid on preserving privacy. And remember, the word 'privacy' was not mentioned by the interviewer; nor was any phrase suggesting privacy. The question put was, 'What do you understand by a "good neighbour"?' or, 'How would you describe a "good neighbour"?' But let us look first at how the English householders regard their neighbours.

I had felt for a long time that the average Englishman considered that the proper place for a neighbour was on his own side of the fence and that most conversations between neighbours were conducted across the fence or hedge or whatever served to mark the boundary of the adjoining property. I was not therefore surprised to learn that many English definitions of a 'good neighbour' included reservations as to the degree of friendliness which would be welcomed by our informants. Thus, one housewife on an English council estate expected her neighbour to be 'friendly without being pushing; kind without being nosey'. In other words, offers of help would be welcomed in an emergency but would be examined carefully for snags or implications at other times. Another, an English husband, after his wife had described her idea of a good neighbour as 'one you can rely on', cut in quickly with, 'Yes, but one you talk to over the fence, but no further than that.' His wife still would not agree: 'I like to invite them in and go to their house,' she said. After a pause, upbringing proved too strong and she also felt obliged to insert a limiting clause, 'but not to get intimate with'.

English householders clearly recognized that neighbours constitute a threat to privacy. In old-established English neighbourhoods, the garden fence effectively marks the physical limits to neighbouring activities and there was much less emphasis on maintaining privacy. Indeed, it became apparent that few had actually suffered from excessive intrusion from neighbours, in the past. Although, in their new homes, the physical barriers were slender in the extreme—in most cases two strands of wire running the length of the garden (yard)—in most people the mental barrier which they had grown up with remained as robust as ever. They tended to keep some new-comers farther apart from their neighbours than they really wanted to be in their new surroundings. Others saw the boundary wire as far too weak a line of defence if the neighbour became 'difficult'. This fear was particularly noticeable amongst the group of working-class people who found themselves on an open-plan council estate, straight from city congestion where close living had helped to make their mental reservations and physical barriers of prime importance. Thus, 'I like being friendly but not too friendly. I don't go into anybody else's home.' This housewife, aged 38 years, had spent all her life in one working-class neighbourhood.

Did these English householders really believe that the main-tenance of a formal or semi-formal barrier of reserve between neighbours was absolutely necessary? Most did, we gathered, but many had put up the barrier on hearsay evidence alone or, more commonly, were continuing the practice of their parents. Very frequently the definition of a good neighbour, who was to be kept to her own side of the fence, was followed by qualifica-tions which suggested that there might be something in having more to do with neighbours, after all. One housewife, aged 31 years with two children, occupying a house (owned) for the first time in her married life, first of all defined a good neigh-bour as '. . . a person who is not inquisitive about other people's affairs. . . . People who are ready to take you at face value.' This was the stereotyped reply but, after a pause, she added, rather wistfully, 'Someone who would help—but we have never done this much—but it would be nice to have a give-and-take arrangement.' She had lived in three furnished apartments in her seven years of married life where neighbours were too close for comfort at times. After two years in her present house she still had not been able to establish a 'give-and-take arrangement', as she called it, with her neighbours.

As stated earlier, American homemakers seemed to possess to a still more marked degree the fear that neighbours might seriously threaten their privacy. Eighteen per cent wanted neighbours to mind their own business and another 14 per cent, making 33 per cent in all, put it a little more mildly and felt that neighbours should not be allowed to get too familiar. These figures are higher than for England and are undoubtedly related to the greater ease of, and the existing pattern for, neighbouring in the United States, an ease which is due as much to physical differences between the two countries as to contrasts in human values, in tradition, outlook and the general way of life.

Over much of the United States, the lowest-cost houses occupied by the lowest-paid workers are set as close as, and often closer than, houses occupied by their opposite numbers on a council housing estate in England. The lowest-cost dwellings to erect—a one-floor plan (bungalow) on a project development —occupy most of the lot (plot). In our survey, the smallest American lots were 50 ft. by 120 ft.

Secondly, in this kind of building development, with bedrooms on the ground floor, the inevitable family car must cause annoyance to neighbours on occasions, especially when there are young children who are reluctant to go to sleep on long, hot summer evenings. 'The driveway of your neighbour is right near your bedroom window': this comment from an American mother showed admirable restraint. By contrast, in England, few families in the lowest income groups have a car and on council estates few houses have a garage or private way; under these conditions the noise of a car engine in high revs. can never be nearer than the highway.

Thirdly, few American lots are fenced in. Yet some residents admitted they would have preferred to fence around their property but feared the strength of public opinion, which in most new neighbourhoods would have been distinctly unfavourable.

Fourthly, although Americans with larger incomes tend to buy larger lots of half an acre or more, they also tend to cover them with larger, low, one-floor-plan houses, two-car garages, car ports, breeze-ways and long drives. In the end there is little

more garden space left on, say, a half-acre plot, than an Englishman would have with his two-storey house on a quarter-
acre plot. The unfortunate American seeking to preserve his
privacy has still not achieved it, and this helps to keep alive the
ambition to achieve a house on a larger lot, farther and farther
out from the city. The attainment or preservation of privacy
seemed to be a major consideration of most American families
interviewed. This was particularly noticeable on the middle-
priced subdivisions. 'Some neighbourhoods are so chummy they
(the neighbours) practically live with you.'

Compared with subdivisions where single lots were developed, relatively less neighbouring was carried out on project
developments and the complaints as to lack of privacy were
more common. The following examples are typical: 'I lie back
until I get to know people before I get too friendly with the
neighbours. Same way at work. Too many come and go to
make friends exactly': this man was a railroad conductor.
Another said, 'We're saving for a fence': this brave man was
self-employed in laying floors. From another project development came the following: 'This is a housing project. Never
again! The houses are too close together. All houses are alike.
This is not the house I want': the man, a plumber, earning
$5,000 (£1,785) a year, bought the house because he could do
so with no down-payment as an 'ex-G.I.' and 'because it was
wonderful for the children'. Previously he had lived in sub-
standard accommodation in a run-down, east side section.
Another, younger, couple hoped to move to a more rural area
to get more peace and quiet for themselves and the children:
'Here television goes on all day from the time when we are
wakened by it in the morning': the husband was a salesman
earning $6,600 (£2,357) a year. 'I have a few neighbours who
are pretty nosey but I think every project has. You can't live
this close without it. We live too close to neighbours. When we
want to yell, we want to yell. We don't like being jammed up': he
was a cabinet-maker with an income of $6,000 (£2,143) a year.

How do the better-off people in America set about guaran-
teeing privacy for themselves? Actually, there are some who
would prefer less privacy. But the majority who wanted more
adopted various devices. One strong-minded household which

had put a fence around their property felt they had to excuse themselves to us and to another local person present—as, no doubt, they had done to the rest of the neighbours—in these terms. The wife's definition of a good neighbour, with which her husband agreed, was 'One who stays in her own yard (garden) until you invite her in. We have fenced in the back yard to keep the dog in.' Admittedly it was a large dog and under State laws dogs were not allowed to roam freely because of a rabies epidemic. Unfortunately, the husband spoiled her subterfuge when he cut in with, 'It stops the children running across the lot. We want privacy.'

Another device we met in America is to build your house in the centre of a lot of one acre or more, when you can say with one householder, 'It's easy (with these large lots) to keep out of one another's hair.' Another went one better. He had tried to solve his problem of securing privacy by buying one and a half acres. He explained, 'We like privacy given by space—but not a fence. We like to withdraw from our neighbours.' To this end, he had set the house back as far from the road as possible and planted a row of shade trees to screen him from both the road and the neighbours. Even so, during the summer they suffered irritation from the 'late-partying' of their neighbours around a swimming-pool. In England, except in remote rural areas, it is only the very well-to-do or the very fortunate, who can afford a plot (lot) big enough to allow them to erect a house in the middle which will be well away from their neighbours. Land values are far too high for the ordinary professional man so to do.

Shade trees are an essential amenity in the gardens of homes throughout most of the United States. Every nurseryman advertises 'shade trees' in the same way as the English nurseryman advertises 'bedding plants'. The people we interviewed were newcomers living in new houses and had been in residence less than four years. But this is long enough for quick-growing trees like sycamore to grow quite large and to 'clothe the plot'. But for the Canadian housewife we interviewed, whose childhood had been spent in England, the privacy they accorded her was still not enough. 'We have privacy with the trees but I want evergreens across the front and a fence across the back with roses.' However, she had lived long enough in the United States to try to excuse herself by adding, 'I have a need to mark my boundaries.' Even she had not reached the point where they contemplated erecting side fences to separate themselves from their neighbours. At this point, it is appropriate to quote an English householder's example of good-neighbourly action: 'Next door, they cut a tree down that was shading us.' This act of neighbourliness in England would have been taken in a reverse sense in the United States.

The 'open-lot' layout of new American subdivisions has been discussed in some detail for two reasons. Firstly, it is radically different from the current practice on comparable new developments in England. Secondly, whilst on both sides of the Atlantic new residents appear to have problems of preserving privacy, they differ somewhat in degree. Concerning boundary fences, English householders appear untroubled by twinges of conscience and allegations of withdrawal from the community. On the contrary, they recognize that this is the norm and, for instance, when a local authority *imposes* an open layout with low, one-foot walls to the road and virtually no division between the plots, council tenants are very concerned and frequently annoyed. Their traditional way of life as town dwellers has led them to accept and expect walls or fences between adjacent residential properties as something right and proper. Except in some parts of New York State, New England and a few industrial areas elsewhere, the average American newcomer to a subdivision, on the other hand, is usually only one generation, at the most, removed from the farm or open-country living. With a garden fence he feels 'fenced in', literally, and since it is alien to his upbringing he feels 'guilty' about it. By contrast, the English newcomer who said, 'We can't keep the children out of the garden; it needs a gate and walls or better fences', was voicing the thoughts of most English people and she did so with no feeling of guilt or shame.[1]

Is this fear of the invasion of privacy justified? What do householders want to keep private? In both countries they seem to want to be able to exchange conversation with their neighbours at all times, and to extend or receive helpful family

[1] Yard or garden fences are commonly met in California, however.

services in times of emergency. In both countries they fear 'noseyness' from neighbours by which, presumably, they mean that the neighbours might discover, by accident if not by design, information about the family way of life which they would not especially like communicated to others.

We have already said that in some English homes, particularly the poorest, there was also the fear that neighbours would come borrowing too often. Whilst the exchange of garden tools was accepted as natural, borrowing food or household items was, in general, not welcomed. To the least well-off householders this suggested bad management of the weekly wage packet with the consequences of which many had been familiar in their previous neighbourhood. In general, one can say that, in England, borrowing between neighbours is deplored and many housewives would go without rather than borrow milk or sugar, for example.

For American readers it should be explained that with little inconvenience an English housewife can walk along to the corner shop to make good any deficiency in her larder and that, quite commonly, she would do *some* shopping on at least three days in every week. The American housewife living on a new subdivision has no corner shop. She shops in the car probably only once a week and to get a single item at other times is not always easy and may prove quite difficult. Surprisingly to my wife and me, a minister's definition of good neighbouring in America included 'women borrowing from each other, for example, a cup of sugar or a bit of salt'. An English minister would never have made this statement. In a retail store at Sheridan (Wyoming), we saw customers buying *sacks* of sugar. At another counter was the largest packet of detergent powder we had ever seen in our lives: it stood as high as a kitchen table. Shopping in bulk is a necessity when your farm is fifty miles from the nearest store; this kind of situation obtains over large areas of the United States and it is with this pattern of buying which many present-day town Americans were brought up. When borrowing from your neighbour is a necessity it is not regarded as a vice, or admission of weakness, but a neighbourly act and this feeling seems to persist in America even where the conditions of supply make it less necessary.

Whilst the fear of prying neighbours was constantly referred to, only two American and four English families admitted that they had suffered from this nuisance. This suggests that the fear was either based on slender foundations or that neutralizing measures had proved effective.

A similar observation can be applied to the complaint of noisy neighbours. Only three American and four English families instanced serious annoyance from noisy neighbours.

Frustrations and Irritations

The most frequently-voiced irritation or frustration came from the lowest-cost American subdivisions and from the lowest-cost English dwellings, or council houses, to the effect that too large a number of houses had been built on too small a plot or lot.

In both countries the unnecessary noise made by neighbours' radio sets was referred to. Only one, and that an American living in the lowest-cost houses, was worried that *his* own record player, or his own organ playing, might interfere with his neighbour: 'We would like to be more private. We would like to have wider lots,' he said.

On two of the higher-priced American subdivisions *four* families, out of forty, did little neighbouring. Three were working-class by origin or occupation. They knew that they were different and they felt constrained to explain in words which usually ran as follows: 'Some are continually neighbouring. Others are happy in their homes—that's us. Neither of us are joiners.' In this case, the husband was a foreman storekeeper and was 'out of his class' compared with his neighbours as regards occupation and way of life, including home furnishing, children's dress, etc., but not as to income which was well up to the average for the subdivision. They had made no friends and the wife had little to do with her neighbours.

By contrast, some of the young professional people living in the lowest-cost American homes were clearly not *en rapport* with their neighbours because of their superior advantages of upbringing and education. In general, these found the close living of the 'project' kind of real-estate development rather confining. One, a housewife, was quite honest as to her attitude to her neighbours, 'I am intolerant of people who have less than average intellect. I don't neighbour myself—others visit me.' Referring to the closeness of the houses she said, 'It squashes individuality. I want more of peace of mind and quietness.' Unfortunately, for her, her extrovert salesman husband did not agree; for him, the close proximity of neighbours was friendly and pleasant. His business took him away from the home all day and many evenings as well and he might have felt differently had he spent as much time in the home as his wife.

This lack of accord between neighbours, seemingly largely due to class consciousness, was noticeable on the higher-priced subdivisions in America. 'Some of the older residents are our best friends. Some of the new ones are trying to put it on. They look for friends in the higher (income) brackets. People in the older homes are not used to this.' This was a well-established professional man who had no need to feel personally inferior: he built his home on one of the first lots to be developed. A similar attitude, in reverse, showed up on an English private-enterprise estate: 'Some come from low-class districts. They give themselves away. They don't mix. They try to make friends but it doesn't last.'

A mother of four children on an English council estate said, 'There are a lot of snobby ones round here. People look down on us because we have so many children.' She was 31 years of age and her husband was 43 and, although they had lived on the estate for two years, she seemed to have been unable to adjust herself to the new neighbourhood. This was well illustrated by her definition of a good neighbour as 'Someone who is willing to give a hand when needed in illness. We have just experienced that. Nobody came then. You'd get a house full in Bedminster', i.e. the old neighbourhood in which she had been brought up. It may be that the poor woman was unlucky in her immediate neighbours or that she found difficulty in making friends because of her own personality. But, although this housewife expressed her views more strongly than the others, it was obvious from the interviews that four children in the family seriously interfered with the mother's ability to spend time with her neighbours. In this sense, having more than the average number of children helped to set the household apart from the rest of the neighbourhood. In coming to this conclusion it is very difficult to evaluate other factors such as social status. But, on American subdivisions, there were eight families with four children or more; of these, six showed some lack of adjustment, i.e. were not quite so close to their neighbours as families with two children, say. The observation of one, a professional worker with a higher than average salary in the $10–15,000 (£3,571–£5,357) a year group, was made with sufficient expression to indicate this feeling of being apart: 'We look on neighbours as acquaintances rather than intimate friends.' A working-class family put it differently: 'We are content *in our home*.'

It must not be deduced from the above that people with larger families are singled out by their neighbours and deliberately set apart. There was no evidence that this was so in either America or England yet some parents with several children appeared apprehensive that this might happen. An English housewife on a private-enterprise estate betrayed the fear when describing what good neighbours she had: 'They don't get disturbed about the boys'; she had four: 16, 10, 7 and 4 years of age, respectively. 'They never complain about their noisiness.' Here, the sense of being different clearly came from within the family.

Yet was it solely a question of the number of children or were other factors involved? We did not ask the religion of any of our families but this was *invariably* volunteered during interviews with American, but rarely with English, families. Both of the American families with four children, above, were Roman Catholics, a fact which was mentioned about them by others on the subdivision: 'We are all Methodists (or Protestants) here except . . .' was the way it was usually referred to. Roman Catholic families stand out on an American subdivision in a predominantly Protestant state or locality, if only because the children attend separate schools, which are frequently situated in another neighbourhood. This may seem wrong to an American Protestant who has been brought up in the belief that schools should not be used to indoctrinate children in any religious faith. Furthermore, so much child and teenage social activity is associated with the school and the church that the children of Roman Catholic families may spend the greater part of the time moving in an entirely different group from other

88

children on the subdivision. In fact, where the nearest Roman Catholic church is some distance away, as commonly happens, they spend a great deal of time *away* from the home neighbourhood. The same applies to Roman Catholic mothers who cannot belong to the local church circles where many new acquaintanceships are made. So much store is laid on church attendance, and so much time is given to associated social activities by American families, that the Roman Catholic friend of a Protestant homemaker would not be human if she did not sometimes feel left out of the neighbourhood social life. There are so many activities she is prevented from sharing because of her religion. The same observation applies to Jewish and other minority groups.

In England, differences of religion are less likely to interfere with the formation of friendships or acquaintanceships if only because fewer people attend church or belong to church social activities (see Chapter 10).

Throughout history, man has stood shoulder to shoulder with his neighbours against a common enemy at his gate, and fighting common causes against authority is still an important factor in welding a group of newcomers into a community. On an American subdivision we found that newcomers had set up a militant organization to repel the threat of installing sidewalks and street-lights. In England, the common enemies were the county council which was providing, they considered, inadequate school facilities, on the one hand, and the bus company which was operating inferior bus services, on the other. The American objection to street-lighting and sidewalks was on the score of cost and obsolescence: 'Nobody walks any more—especially after dark' was the cry. The battle waged for several months during which all the men got to know one another at the frequent 'defence' meetings held in one another's homes. Eventually, a decision was reached by the council not to install either and both those who had won the battle and those who had lost felt a glow of civic pride that as a community they had thrashed this problem out together, democratically. Most of them then proceeded to erect their own street-lamps, on their own property somewhere between house and road. The same purpose was served, i.e. to light the front of the house and the lot, but scope was given for individual expression in design—traditional and modern, western-style and Oriental, wood, wrought-iron and concrete—all this, but never the uniformity of local authority street-lamp design which prevails in England.

As frequently happens in England also, one of our American subdivisions was divided between three local authority areas for different services, i.e. an incorporated district (broadly corresponding to an English urban district council territory), a big city and, finally, part was in the area of a township (roughly equivalent to an English rural district council). The city council had acquired a reputation for grabbing rural areas as soon as they became partly built over, at the same time conferring the advantage of city services. Again, as in England, these services were not always rated so highly by the householders who were taken over. Now, the town service most prized by Americans is a good school system, especially when their own children are of school age. But, because its running expenses are defrayed almost entirely from local taxes, local education is very expensive. If you have no children or they are grown up it is understandable if you prefer an authority with a cheaply-run, i.e. usually inferior standard, school system. In this particular subdivision, the incorporated district had an excellent, but expensive ('tax-wise') school system, the city had a good but not so expensive one, and the township area an unpretentious, more cheaply operated school system. In general, Roman Catholics preferred the cheapest local system available because they sent their children out of the area to the nearest Roman Catholic school (in this case in the city) to which they paid tuition fees. Fairly early in the development of this particular subdivision threat of a take-over bid from the city insinuated itself. After a great deal of discussion on the back porch and elsewhere, full agreement between the residents was never achieved and eventually most of the subdivision was annexed to the incorporated district, a little group of four houses went to the big city and a smaller island of three stayed with the township. In fact, some homes paid education taxes to one authority, sanitary taxes to another and water taxes to a third. This obvious (to an American), untidy (to an Englishman), solution seemed to satisfy everyone, and the newcomers were able to relax once more, happy in the knowledge that as a result of the agitation they häd applied democratic processes: in addition they now knew by Christian name almost everyone on the subdivision.

Communal discord is very frequently promoted in an English village when a group of new arrivals threatens to bring urban progress to the village way of life in the form of street-lamps. An application for the service, in a *rural* authority area, must have the majority approval of a parish meeting. This gives opportunities for 'organization' and the side with the best organizing ability usually wins. By contrast, when a group of new houses is built in an area which lies within the jurisdiction of an *urban* district council, street-lighting is installed automatically. Pavements (sidewalks) are invariably provided with new houses on any estate (subdivision) development in England—under both rural and urban district councils. Local agitation is only directed towards these services when their provision is too long delayed.

Although the standard of educational provision does not usually vary sufficiently from one English authority to the next to lead to local differences, the absence of a school *near enough* for the newcomers' children to reach easily very frequently leads to concerted and sometimes vociferous action on the part of new residents. Success in one direction may induce new residents to campaign for other benefits, for example, the provision by the appropriate authority of a playing field, health centre or a library. All these services resulted from, or provision was accelerated by, the organized action of the newcomer community living on one of our English private-enterprise estates. But the occurrence which cemented this local loyalty most firmly of all took place when council approval was given for a hotel in the middle of the residential part of the estate. To add insult, in the view of the residents, a dancing licence was also permitted. The 'Residents Association' which was set up later entered the local political arena and obtained a sizeable share of district council seats at the first local government election it fought.

On one American subdivision, a group of residents discovered that combined action could sometimes misfire and some discontent between neighbours resulted. The homes were arranged in a rough circle and the road which served them

91

circled a patch of ground which at first nobody bothered about and which consequently became a jungle of weeds. Talk led to organization and combined action and the bare patch was 'graded' (levelled) and seeded. But dissension arose as the grass grew; 12 homemakers had played their part in the initial preparations but when we were conducting our interviews only two were sharing the job of cutting it. Voluntary action had initiated co-operation but was not strong enough in this case to sustain it. In England, the need for such action would have been recognized when the layout plans were approved and such a grass area would have been taken over by the local authority, and the roads, pavements and street-lighting put in, automatically. The rateable values of the properties would have been adjusted to accord with these amenities. Dissent on the part of the householders would have availed little. The result on the English pattern would have been eminently satisfactory but more expensive; the Americans result was very unsatisfactory, both visually and as an example of continuing co-operative effort, although its financial cost to the community was negligible.

Finally, there is the, sometimes unvoiced, resentment of newcomers which older residents in the district are betrayed into showing by word, deed or simply a 'sniff' or a toss of the head. This was met on both sides of the Atlantic. Two examples from an English estate illustrate: 'The Yate people refer to us as the people who are from the estate. They are not unfriendly but there is a barrier.' This sentiment emerged on every English estate, both council and private-enterprise. Some residents went farther: 'Local people blame newcomers for the rise in the cost of vegetables, etc. Some regret the loss of rights of way across open country now covered with houses.' In America, similar observations were passed: 'The older residents lost some of the openness to which they had been used for years. The people at the back still regard our lot as their back yard. Children play there and they leave trash in their yard which blows over our yard.'

6

PARTYING

A<small>N</small> American minister of religion, resident on one of our subdivisions, wanted his neighbour to be 'interested but not nosey, one who would be willing to share good fortunes or troubles but who is not in and out all the time'. This fear of many Americans has been dealt with in detail in the section on preserving privacy. We have shown that with many it is more fear than fact; few suffer actual invasion from their neighbours, and some actually would prefer more frequent contact with them. Residents who had come from smaller country towns or villages made this quite plain. One such expressed horror that the neighbours amongst whom he lived 'would object if you dropped in when they were eating their dinner'. 'What of it!' he exclaimed. I can hear many Americans saying, 'and so would I', for in most neighbourhoods a visitor would be expected to telephone before doing so, even if he lived just across the street. Not so the country-bred American or, indeed, the telephone-less Englishman. This particular householder was seriously considering moving because he could not find the kind of neighbourliness to which he had been accustomed when he lived in a small town some 30 miles away where, incidentally, he was amongst people with whom he had lived and worked for many years. When he arrived on the new subdivision the neighbours across the street had welcomed him the first afternoon with a freshly-cooked pumpkin pie. This gesture he welcomed as admirable, but, although, subsequently, he had found his neighbours friendly 'in the yard', he had failed to persuade them to cross his threshold. He had himself entered their home on divers excuses but had met a blank wall whenever he had tried to develop the acquaintanceship farther. 'People here are not socially minded,' he remarked rather bitterly. The man himself was a member of a profession which is highly respected and he enjoyed an income slightly above the average for the subdivision. His manner was naturally easy and there appeared no obvious reason why his efforts to make friends should have been repulsed. On the same subdivision a homemaker from one of the western, prairie, states said that she, similarly, missed the kind of open friendliness she had known at home. She had tried hard by organizing parties for children and adults, several in her own home: these appeared to have been well attended, but reciprocal action just did not take place. On this better-class estate, occupied in the main by householders over 35 years, she had failed signally to recreate the habit of 'dropping in' she knew so well in her youth.

In England, on our evidence, calling on neighbours unannounced is not considered a virtue either and steps are quickly taken to curb excessive neighbouring of this kind at least on a relatively newly-built estate. Yet, while interviewing in the United States, we were told a dozen times 'some neighbourhoods are so chummy they practically live with you'. Some of our informants put this forward as evidence of a good community spirit but they were usually the younger people on lower—but never on the lowest-cost—housing developments.

'Block' parties were typical of this kind of moderately-priced subdivision. We were told many times, and from observations and, indeed, participation we believe it to be true, that for most citizens of the United States, any excuse is good enough reason for a party. A party almost always includes eating. Use of the word 'block' in this sense is usually intended to embrace the whole of a short street or that part of a long street from one side-street to the next. In the long, summer holiday months parents frequently get together with their children and have picnic meals out of doors. Since there are seldom boundary fences between the properties, and because the climate does not encourage English-type flower gardening, American yards mainly comprise stretches of very tough grass which is resistant to hot sun and to young feet. One yard appears to run into the next and several adjacent yards on a new subdivision give the appearance of a single large lawn. As the years pass, and because shrubs and trees grow so rapidly, individual lots stand out from each other yet appear to merge. Some yards will have swings and similar games equipment.[1] This open kind of layout is ideally suited to communally-organized picnics which can overflow quite easily from yard to yard and basement to basement if the weather turns wet, assuming that there is a preponderance of families with young children, and young wives who are energetic and able to cook the enormous quantities of food demanded of them by healthy appetites; hamburgers, wieners (sausages), potato salads; blueberry pies and so on according to season.

To quote one young American mother, on a medium-priced subdivision, 'On a holiday we have a whole big picnic.—We are really a sociable group on Stafford—we have cooking out in large groups—the men play volley-ball in our yards.' Apparently specialization creeps in: 'On the block east of us they square-dance together. We get together for cook-outs', i.e. for out-door cooking described above.

This block-party kind of neighbouring appeared to flourish in areas of young middle-income families partly because so many of the husbands were away 'travelling the State' as salesmen, State officials, etc., and wives were left with time and children on their hands. It was less apparent in the areas of cheaper houses where some 12 per cent of homemakers (housewives) were out to work during the day. In the areas of better-class housing, families, parents and children, tended to be older and included a higher proportion of teenagers for whom there was a wealth of organized activity associated with schools, churches, etc. Furthermore, we were told an increasing proportion of wives in the better estates take up some part-time work in middle age when their children are no longer round their skirts, or in summer their shorts or slacks which seem to be worn by women in the house, at the super-market and almost everywhere except to church.

The comments of the grown-up daughter of one of our homemakers, who was present throughout the interview, is relevant to this statement: 'Most of my friends' mothers got jobs when

[1] On more-expensive subdivisions private swimming pools are not uncommon.

we were going into college.' At this her mother explained that 'I *needed* to do something (to occupy her day) and this is a very satisfying job' (she was employed part-time in a medical re-habilitation centre). But her husband did not quite like the ex-planation and insisted, 'But you were influenced by the cost of the girls' education which pushed the budget above my salary.'

The kind of neighbouring described above is typical of *new* housing developments elsewhere in the United States but it is not typical of older settled areas, even those which adjoined two of the subdivisions used for our survey as the two following comments demonstrate: 'Visiting back and forth in the old vil-lage (of Worthington) is nil. (This neighbourhood) is not typical of the rest of Worthington.' A couple in an older house nearby explained, 'We do not need to socialize any more.' How like England and the English these two comments from Ameri-cans seem.

Coffee Parties

The importance of the coffee party in the life of American women is difficult adequately to describe to an Englishwoman in whose way of life it has no counterpart. It is true that several English housewives regretted that there was no restaurant nearer than the city centre where they could have had a cup of coffee with a friend. This came from women who lived on private-enterprise estates and never from council-house tenants. The suggestion that a dozen or more neighbours might get together in their own homes during the morning or afternoon for a coffee party was completely outside their experience. For the average Englishwoman, taking cups of coffee in the morning or tea in the afternoon is a largely middle-class activity which you indulge in before you are married, or in the early years of married life when you are not too busy before the children arrive on the scene. Once you have a family you usually have to forego such interesting pleasures for a number of reasons, to which those related to cost and mobility are important.

Americans visiting England miss the drug-store snack bar as much as any other facility although they express themselves as 'crazy' about English teashops. Commercial coffee bars have only relatively recently gained a hold on the British public. They arrived first as a substitute for working-class restaurants, i.e. as cheap snack bars. Later they became haunts of teenagers. They have only recently become 'respectable' for adults. Few are to be found in the neighbourhood shopping centres on the fringe of cities, i.e. where newcomers might take or meet friends.

The custom of taking 'afternoon tea', the kind which was daintily served by trim maids in cap and apron in some Victorian drawing-rooms, has never been as prevalent in England as many Americans believe. The number of homes where this custom is still upheld is few and declining, but in many households, of all classes, a more substantial tea takes the place of the evening meal on Saturday and Sunday at least. On these two days the main meal can be eaten at midday because the whole family is able to assemble. Tea at four or five o'clock allows the teenage members of the family to leave early for the cinema or some other Saturday evening social activity. Afternoon tea has never been the social occasion for the working or professional classes which our American cousins have gathered from English books, films and plays.

For a number of reasons, the English housewife has less time to spare for morning or afternoon coffee or similar social gatherings even if she wished or could afford them, and from considerations of cost many of those interviewed could not have participated so on the scale which the American hostess expects to provide. The subject of the time available for neighbouring is dealt with more fully elsewhere.

Furthermore, had she the time the English housewife has not the transport. As we have seen, not all families had two cars in America although several had three. But, only two wives could not drive and in most instances where only one car was maintained this was available when the wife needed it, usually quite frequently we found, for special needs such as attending a social gathering or doing the weekly shopping at the supermarket. Either the wife drove the husband to work and kept the car for the day, the husband belonged to a car pool, or he was able to ride with a nearby workmate. When the wife held a job as well, if only a part-time one, she invariably ran a car of her own. By contrast, the English housewife enjoys no such easy mobility; journeys by public transport can be tiring for her and, as we were told repeatedly in the enquiry, expensive so that maintaining contact with friends who lived in another neighbourhood was frequently difficult. The cultivation of new ones at any distance was mostly impossible.

The American homemaker has been brought up on coffee and 'cokes'—since she was a teenager. At one interview a 12-year-old youngster complained bitterly about the lack of amenities on the subdivision. 'Why! there's no drug-store where the kids can meet when they've got nothing else to do. Up in Worthington (the nearest shopping centre, one and a half to two miles away) there are three or four drug-stores where all the kids meet and talk.' Had drug-stores been in the experience of our English teenagers they would have echoed these sentiments for there are all too few places in new English neighbourhoods for youngsters to meet informally.

Coffee at the 'Dairy Queen', 'Howard Johnson' or similar restaurants, which occur on all the main highways and 'thru' ways' when on long journeys with 'pop' and 'mom'; coffee at the 'Teen Stop' or similar youth gathering at the church or the school society; coffee in the fraternity or sorority house at college; coffee with business acquaintances; and finally coffee with the neighbours. This last my wife and I found fascinating, perhaps because it was so different from anything we had met in England and perhaps because we envied the speed with which neighbours were able to 'get acquainted' through the everyday action of drinking a simply-prepared non-alcoholic beverage.

'All we need is the excuse for a party and there is a party . . . men and women, young and old. . . . It starts from the age of 12 upwards. This change has taken place over the last twenty years. We did not do it when I was a youngster.' This came from an 'elderly' American father of 35 years. For many women the best excuse of all to get together with the neighbours around is the departure of an old neighbour or the arrival of a new one. In one street on one of the better-class subdivisions the first house was put up by the realtor (estate agent) for his own occupation. His wife gave a coffee party for the first two or three new

families within a day or so of their arrival and, gradually, it became the custom for the last arrival but one to hold the party
in her home for the next newcomer. All the neighbours in the
street were invited and they arranged amongst themselves, over
the telephone of course, for every American home has a telephone, who was to bake the pie—who to make the cakes, etc.
We found that later comers knew nothing of the origins of this
custom. For them, 'People rallied round and had an afternoon
coffee for me. When the next lady moved in I had one for her'
was the way it was usually explained. Put at its lowest, everybody learnt something about the newcomer, her name, the
number in her family, the sort of home she had, something of
her earlier life, and older residents were able to hazard a guess
as to what sort of a neighbour she was going to be. For her part,
the newcomer became *immediately* acquainted with all the people
around her, learnt a great deal about the community and the
locality in a very short time: the good shops for groceries, the
best hairdresser, available teenager activities and the like.
When subsequently she went into her yard she did not have the
feeling that her neighbours were spying on her from behind the
curtains (as so many English housewives had reported) to try
and find out what she was like. They already knew something
about her from that first coffee party. They would get to know
more as fresh families arrived, which on a new subdivision meant
every month or less. In this fashion the whole 'block' became
welded into a community.

Properties change hands more frequently in the United
States, for the reason given elsewhere in the text, and so there
were still excuses for neighbourly gatherings even after the first
flush of new arrivals. One public-spirited homemaker in another
part of the same subdivision—a woman of 50 years with two
grown-up daughters and a part-time job of her own—still felt
that people seemed a little slow at getting to know each other
and that she ought to do something about it. She had had eight
moves in 34 years occasioned by shifts in her husband's employment. 'I had times of being lonely and when we came here I did
something about it.' Her 'something' was to give a coffee party
immediately and to repeat it once a year for all the women in
the street; since it was a long street this meant more than thirty

people. Like most American homes of this income group the living-room or lounge was large, 30 ft. by 16 ft. plus, and there was a dining area, or family room, of the same size. The two were linked by a very wide archway. Between the family room and the kitchen there was a bar past which guests filed when 'mother had a coffee'. Her daughter said, 'All mother's parties finish up in the family room with mother behind the bar. We Americans feed on the cafeteria system.' She was not quite correct; some do but many do not: only a minority, less than 10 per cent, had a breakfast bar. From our observations we are less inclined to believe her general statement as being true of all or most American families. Admittedly, breakfast is a 'catch or grab' meal as it is in many English homes, and almost all American kitchens we inspected were furnished with a table or a bar at which meals could be served. This practice is, of course, becoming more prevalent in new homes in England, also. In homes where teenagers determine the daily meal routine the two other meals of the day are more likely to be more casually eaten than in England because of the great number of activities indulged in by American youngsters. But, in younger families where the children were, say, between the ages of 3 and 12, it was frequently emphasized to us that evening meals, at least, were eaten in the sitting room, family room or dining annex, as appropriate, as part of general family training and discipline. There were some indications that during the long days of high summer this routine was honoured in theory rather than in its practice.

It should not be concluded from the description of 'partying', above, that regular and frequent coffee parties between neighbours are typical of all, or even of all new, subdivisions. An American homemaker, 35 years of age, who was happily occupying her second home since marriage, nevertheless, looked back with some nostalgia to the free-and-easy gatherings she remembered in her first home, when she was one of a group of young married women and 'all the gals got together for coffee'. She was on very good terms with her present neighbours but she missed the close intimacy she had built up in her last neighbourhood peopled mainly with other young, hard-up, professional families. She was perhaps unfortunate in her immediate neighbours for we acquired no evidence to show that coffee parties were more numerous amongst young homemakers than middle-aged ones, or that middle-priced subdivisions indulged in the activity more than better-priced ones. But, the practice of coffee drinking clearly does vary with the subdivision and the people who live there.

Whilst the coffee-party formula is used widely in America, most newcomers develop friendships and find new acquaintances from an area wider than the immediate neighbourhood or sub-division on which they reside. They meet new faces in church, at school or through the activities associated with cultural or athletic sports organizations. Eventually, for some people this may mean that there is less time left for neighbouring or gossip-ing over morning coffee. 'At Colonial Hills there is too much of this', i.e. gossiping over cups of coffee. This homemaker now had cups of coffee in the morning with one or two neighbours at a time. 'At Colonial Hills (her last neighbourhood) people wasted too much of the day talking.'

For many American families a large living-room with labour-saving devices for the easy issue of food to large numbers of guests is absolutely essential. Church circle parties, cultural or specialist interest group parties and neighbour parties may each comprise upwards of 30 participants. By English standards our own lounge or sitting room, with dining-annex, which is an L-shaped room of 25 ft. total length and 15 ft. at its widest, is large, but my wife would hesitate to crowd 30 people in it at one time: yet this we found to be a common practice in America.

With this free-and-easy coffee-party kind of introduction to one's neighbours it is easy to appreciate the opportunities for abuse and the fear of infringement of privacy, which was so noticeable amongst American families. In some streets we found that the early neighbour coffee parties had served their purpose and none had been held for a whole year. 'We used to have family cook-outs in the first two years but not now.' Most of the homes on this subdivision had been erected two or three years earlier. At first, the families had welcomed the opportunities of becoming acquainted with each other but had moved on to develop other forms of social activity which sometimes did, and sometimes did not, include their neighbours. Some early acquaintanceships developed into closer friendship. This was illustrated by the mother, above, who in talking later about her son's friend added, 'I think a lot of his mother and "visit" a lot with her on the telephone.'

Americans appear always ready to move house with change of job or improved economic position. Young professional men with good prospects are not at all averse to buying homes on project developments of the lowest cost. On the lowest-cost housing project 12 of the 20 husbands interviewed were under 30 years of age, compared with none (out of the 40) on the two most-expensive subdivisions. Young professional Americans seem less inclined to hang large mortgage repayments around their necks, large that is relative to their income. This is not exactly from free choice. Unless the house is on a project approved for a G.I. loan, i.e. the lowest-cost housing, in our experience a purchaser had to find one-third of the purchase price. That is a high proportion compared with the 10 per cent of the average British building society loan. It means that, in America, more young professional men are found on projects living side by side with skilled and unskilled artisans who often earn more than they do. But as soon as the young professional improves his economic position, or, as he says, 'has acquired enough equity', he sells the house and buys another one in a better-class neighbourhood, partly as a status symbol American sociologists tell us. [Some realtors (estate agents) are prepared to carry through a part-exchange transaction accepting the old house as a deposit on the new.] Be that as it may, from our observations many young Americans move for reasons other than the achievement of social status. Some families had owned and lived in three homes in ten years whilst still at the same work place. In the early days they had lived in homes which were clearly inadequate or inconvenient—but inexpensive. They moved to better homes as soon as they could afford to do so because they knew that they and their families would lead better lives by doing so. The achievement of status may have entered into their decisions but this was clearly incidental and less important than securing more rooms, more privacy or better schooling for their children. The young ambitious types in the earlier phases of their careers who were living on lowest-cost subdivisions passed remarks like, 'Generally speaking people are only stopping over here.' Few young professional families living on the cheapest projects seemed completely at ease in their temporary locations: 'We have no privacy here. The neighbours are within earshot.'

Some of the artisans who start on the same project development as the young salesman or teacher climb a similar ladder, if more slowly. Thus, on two of the best estates three men (out of 40) described themselves as assistant managers, but whom I suspect in England would have been termed foremen. For example, one man was one of three assistants to the service manager of a large retail automobile business. His annual income of $10,000 (£3,574) was as high as some of his professional neighbours and he had a cottage and a boat on Lake Erie, two hundred miles away, which he visited each weekend. Another artisan who described himself as 'in management' said of his neighbours, 'Most are college graduates. My neighbours play golf but I like flowers.' He graduated from High School but did not go on to college. He talked with his neighbours and mowed their lawns when they were on holiday but clearly had relatively little to do with them socially on other occasions. It was noticeable that his neighbours in the same street whom we interviewed never referred to him in conversation with us, even when conversation was deliberately led in that direction. They were all aware of the man's occupation because he parked his firm's truck on his drive each evening. 'We are all college graduates around here' was the tenor of their replies, also. By contrast, they were not backward in claiming acquaintance with the bank manager, the successful salesman or the attorney who were also neighbours.

The wife of the motor-service engineer seemed similarly withdrawn from her neighbours, all of whom she knew by name, mainly because she was secretary of a church circle. Her definition of a good neighbour revealed more than she appreciated. She liked neighbours to 'co-operate' by which she meant controlling their dogs and their children both of whom, apparently, disturbed her shrubs. She liked neighbours to be 'not "overly" noisy. I don't like ribaldry. They should leave each other alone and not run in and bother me if I'm busy.'

Less-enterprising artisans remain on their project which, be-cause of the rapid change-over, very quickly becomes populated with others of their kind or by birds of passage, such as hard-up married students who rent the homes. Over the years, a neigh-bourly spirit develops but, at the outset, on these lowest-priced projects there are no neighbouring coffee parties and, as in England, it takes longer to get to know your neighbour. The absence of neighbouring here is not easy to explain. Shortage of money is not the main reason because working-class people are relatively well paid in the United States, that is relative to pro-fessional workers in their own country. A quarter of all house-wives on the two lowest-priced subdivisions went out to work and this must have been a contributory cause. Very few adults on the two cheapest subdivisions belonged to a church club or circle, where they might have met neighbours and friends. There was no tradition of welcoming coffee-parties; these appear to be mainly a middle-class and not a working-class activity. But, whatever the reason, suspicion of their neighbours seemed to be much stronger amongst the occupants of the lower-cost houses than amongst the professionals.

On these low-cost subdivisions it was found that the most im-portant avenue of approach to neighbours was through the children. One man, a mechanic, who possessed a marked sense of community, got to know four of his neighbours reasonably well in this way. 'We fixed a horse-shoe court[1]—but we don't socialize here.' None of the parents he had come to know in this way had been into his house even for a cup of coffee. 'I knew the children before I knew the father or mother. They (the children) come and watch in the yard while I am working.' He had 'fixed' his neighbour's lawn-mower, however. In fact, most of the families became acquainted with one another in this way, via the children and through the fathers who hailed each other in the yard or the street and opened acquaintanceships by bor-rowing one another's tools. Acquaintance with neighbours appeared to come through the homemaker (housewife) only infrequently on the lowest-cost American subdivision.

[1] For English readers this game is a cross between bowls and quoits and is played by throwing a horse-shoe.

Afternoon Tea, Evening Coffee and the Evening Meal

In America the evening meal is usually eaten at about 6 or
6.30 p.m. and is the main meal of the day. It is a substantial
repast even in the hottest weather, at which, if you are enter-
tained by friends, substantial helpings of freshly-cooked meat
and vegetables are followed by huge helpings of pie or fresh fruit
and ice cream, biscuits, cheese and anything else in season, or
out of season locally, since the wide range of climate of the
U.S.A., its huge canning industry and efficient marketing
bring a great range of food products to the table. But the evening meal in America is for the family or for entertaining friends
or special visitors. Neighbours are not normally included in this,
unless they have become, or are on the way to becoming, close
friends. 'We visit (neighbours) but we know what time the husband comes home and we try not to stay too long to make it
difficult for her to get the dinner ready.'

In England, the main meal may be at mid-day, especially if
the children are at school and come home for lunch, which is
still called dinner in artisan homes. Father has a special, 'hot'
meal prepared but the children and mother will usually take
tea, i.e. bread and butter and cake, but not a cooked savoury
meal. In some parts of the Midlands and the north of England
high tea is served; this comprises a savoury dish supported
by bread and butter, jam and cake. An evening meal is eaten
in many middle-class homes where it is served between seven
and eight o'clock, a custom which may stem from the evening
'dinner' of the upper-middle and wealthy class. It is especially
common when the father, a professional man, is a commuter
and arrives home fairly late in the evening. It is quite usual
for close friends to be invited to share this meal. By contrast,
in working-class homes close friends would usually be invited
to a meal on Saturday or Sunday. This would be to tea and
not an evening meal; it would be a special tea with an array
of cakes, tarts, jellies, stewed fruit and the like.

In English homes where a cooked evening meal is regularly
prepared it will be much less ambitious than that prepared by
the American housewife. Neighbours would not be invited to
share it. Since the English meal of the late afternoon or early

evening is 'lighter' than the American one about this time, there is more scope for another but simpler meal to be served later in the evening. Inviting friends in 'for a cup of coffee', which usually includes sandwiches, cakes and some special dessert dish, is quite common amongst professional people in England and the practice appears to be moving down the social ladder. The invitation to coffee is an excuse for friendly conversational exchanges. To such gatherings neighbours who are known, or whom a family wishes to get to know better, may be invited. This late evening meal does not appear to have its counterpart in the United States.

Cups of tea and coffee at all hours of the day are much more common in England than America: thus, the definition of a good neighbour given by one working-class English housewife was, 'Someone who is pleasant and will have a cup of tea with you.' She was still a little apprehensive of her neighbours, however, and added '. . . but does not want to know all your business.' The cup of tea she was thinking of would more likely rest on the corner of the kitchen table than be served in the best parlour.

Tea is brewed in the English home much more, and coffee much less frequently, than in America, although the consumption of coffee is increasing. In most English homes it is customary to 'make', 'mash' or 'brew' a cup of tea or coffee about eleven in the morning, about four in the afternoon and at any time in the evening from eight o'clock onwards. Any visitor—a close friend or a casual caller—is invited to share this, and the time of its preparation may be advanced or delayed according to a visitor's arrival, the television programme, the time of the previous meal or, in summer, the stage reached in gardening activity. In an American home you are offered a hard or soft drink according to age, sex or the host's estimate of your experience. The refreshment appears before the guest in a couple of seconds since the preparations associated with the making of fresh tea or coffee are not involved. Substitutes such as that abomination (to an Englishman) 'instant tea' would not be tolerated by a self-respecting English housewife who would feel she was letting herself down in the eyes of the visitor, if she was not being downright casual. The preparation of the English pot of tea, just because it involves this organization, is much more a social experience than the offer of a glass of coca cola or iced tea.[1] For this reason, to invite a neighbour into the house for a cup of tea or coffee suggests that you are looking beyond the traditional conception of a neighbour and are prepared to treat the person as a friend.

This social 'overtone' is not implied when an American homemaker invites neighbours in for a 'coke' or a coffee. As one said: 'We wives can call one another on the telephone and say "How about a 'coke' (or a coffee)" and before you know where you are you are visiting', i.e. on talking terms with them. No close friendship, present or potential, need be implied in such an invitation, as would be the case if an English housewife performed a similar action and invited her neighbour in for a cup of tea. This simple yet effective avenue of getting acquainted with neighbours is virtually closed to the English housewife—especially the working-class housewife. 'When I go out to hang up my clothes (washing) I see my neighbour and in no time at all we end up having coffee together,' said an American homemaker. The English housewife does not, one could say cannot, do this. It is just not done. As one said, rather wistfully, 'I have got to know them all (the neighbours) but I have never been into anybody's house.' She had lived there for four years but might have lived there for twenty for all the hope she had of breaking down the natural reserve of her neighbours on this council estate. Quite clearly, she herself never imagined that she could ever get past this barrier and, indeed, could scarcely bring herself to put her need into words; her voice alone betrayed her. One housewife, and only one, held the American view which she expressed in the following words: 'A good neighbour comes in and invites you for a cup of tea when you've got a spare moment. She might say, "Let's go for a walk", or "Let's go to the shops today". . . . You know, very nice and neighbourly. . . . You don't feel lonely that way.' One other had successfully broken down the barrier: 'We often have cups of tea together.'

---

[1] 'Iced tea' comprises the dregs of several brewings of tea kept cool in the refrigerator. A sprig of mint is hung on the lip of the glass: sometimes a slice of lemon replaces the mint. Either of these drinks can be obtained in a restaurant or drugstore.

Partying

At holiday times, especcially in the autumn and winter, it is the practice for American families to throw out a general invitation to their neighbours informng them that they are having an 'open house' and that all will be welcome to refreshment and conversation. We were told repeatedly 'At Christmas there were three "open houses" in this street'; there were only ten homes in all. In this home the wife said, 'All new people are anxious to become better acquainted. In an older neighbourhood, neighbours are less anxious because they have established friends.' Of this comment on older neighbourhoods I cannot write with the same authority, since all the families formally interviewed for the enquiry were newcomers, but questioning old-established families elsewhere it appeared that friends and well-known neighbours were frequently expected to gather round, say, at Christmas and Thanksgiving. The only difference in the new homes was that neighbours who were known only slightly were welcomed. Children are included in the invitations and may gather in the basement of one home which has been 'done over' by the householder as a children's play room. Explaining this, one mother said, 'My husband gets a collection of slides from art galleries to show to the kids at parties.' Another showed his 35-millimetre camera slides to youthful audiences.

In England, the custom of keeping 'open house' has mainly been confined to country living and even there is dying if not dead. In Scotland, the practice of 'first footing' at New Year is a survival of this ancient practice of neighbouring at time of festival. If, as one would suspect, the 'open house' custom finds its roots in rural living, one would expect American townsmen to indulge in it more than English townsmen because a much higher proportion is only a generation or so removed from the farm.

It is hard to reconcile the practice of American 'open house' festivities with the often expressed fear of intrusion from neighbours. However, here the American host has a certain advantage over an English one. Few Americans possess the kind of reserve, common to most Englishmen, which causes them to hold back from any situation which might conceivably lead to some future embarrassment. A personal example will illustrate this. An American host shows little hesitation in indicating to his guests when the time has arrived, in his view, for them to leave for home. When this occurs the guests do not appear to take offence as they certainly would in England. They may sometimes be rather relieved that the decision has been taken for them. By contrast, however late the guests linger, the English host may not give the slightest indication that he expects them to depart. To do so would be considered the height of bad form and would in many instances be followed by a rift in the pattern of friendly visits. Since writing this paragraph I have enjoyed the hospitality of the Deep South and hasten to add that the Southern host, even when he hails from the North, is more akin to the Englishman in this respect. Southern hospitality is more 'Southern European' than American; a greater variety of food and drink—especially alcoholic—light-hearted as well as serious conversation and, altogether, an easier pattern of social relationships are typical.

7

FRIENDS OLD AND NEW

'I DON'T like *neighbours*. I just keep to one close neighbour. A good neighbour is one you can rely on . . . that you can tell anything to without its going farther.' This working-class English housewife on a council estate was 21 years of age with a child of 2½ years. Clearly, she missed the advice and friendliness of her mother and her mother's friends for she continued: 'One who helps you when you haven't any money. These were the kind of people near my mother's home where we used to live.' She wanted a friend badly for she had not yet learnt to stand on her own feet.

It seemed to be the general opinion on English council estates that you might know many of your neighbours by name but you needed only one real friend. In general, house-wives who had made one fairly close friend of a neighbour seemed much happier and more contented than those who had not. They walked up to the shops together, met one another's children from school, or did an occasional baby-sitting duty although there is less need for this now that so many homes have a television set, which also left less spare cash for outings.

Quite a number of English housewives, however, had failed to find a friend nearby even when they actually recognized the need to do so. Some were worried by this. For example: 'In Birmingham, I had a real friend in my neighbour. We went out together. We go back and stay with them.' The husband agreed, wistfully: 'We have no close friends here', to which his wife added: 'If we moved I should not be thinking of them (i.e. the new neighbours).' As our interviewer commented later,

'Although they had lived in the house three years they have not yet put down their roots.'

Making new friends is a very personal affair and the ability to do so varies greatly with the individual. One English house-wife was able to say, 'I have made more friends in a year at Yate than all the time I was in Bristol', but she was unusual. She had recognized, quite early, that it was too far for her friends to visit her frequently and she set out deliberately to fill the gap by making new ones. Some of her neighbours would have been happier had they followed her example. The men do not seem to need the companionship of close friends to the same extent. No doubt many find this satisfaction in their places of employment; most seemed only to want their homes and their garden.

Besides the general suspicion with which so many people initially regard their neighbours, on a new English housing estate opportunities for getting to know neighbours really well are, as has been shown, limited. In the first place, you have to find a family with fairly similar interests to your own. Two families on one private-enterprise estate who had succeeded in doing this 'lived in the same style of house and were, therefore, in the same income level' the husband said. (He did not realize how widely family incomes can vary amongst occupants of similar houses.) But he continued, 'They have a similar young family and therefore the same outlook. This is important to us because we are strangers to the district.' 'This is the very first time I've lived on a housing estate and I found it a bit strange at first,' added the wife. Perhaps the best example of 'good neighbours turned friends' was described by a couple who were soon to move to another town to which the husband was being transferred by his firm. 'I would like to take my neighbour with me. She takes in goods delivered to the door. We exchange garden tools, roller, cutter, etc.; we mow the lawns alternately.' The husbands attended the same evening institute classes together whilst the wives 'share cups of tea'. They got one another's shopping and took in the washing when it rained. This sense of complete accord with another family was rarely met in England and a council housewife summed up the situa-tion for most newcomers: 'There's no way of becoming friendly

Friends Old and New

with the Warmley people.' Her neighbours were 'good' but
they were not the kind she wanted to make close friends of.

We have shown that the American way of life offers many
more opportunities for getting to know your neighbours well
enough to turn them into close friends if the need is felt—
through 'block' parties ard general neighbouring, extra-
curricular school activities, church attendance and in general
social events. Yet relatively few American families appeared
to have made close friends on their new subdivision. Those
newcomers who had made new friends, as contrasted with
acquaintances, comprised 10 per cent of all families in America
and 9 per cent in England. The question, 'Where do your best
friends live?' was asked at all interviews on two American
subdivisions. One quarter replied without hesitation that they
were to be found in other parts of the city of Columbus and its
suburbs. One quarter said they had made new friends locally,
although not all on the same subdivision, and the remaining
half seemed to experience difficulty in answering the question
because of their inability to distinguish between friends and
acquaintances.

Those who kept up friendship with families in other parts of
the town had first met one another in a wide variety of ways
—through work, church, earlier places of residence. Many were
friends of long standing, for example made at school or college.
'All our friends are at Delaware' (20 miles away). 'My real
friends are at Hillsboro, Ohio' (75 miles away). 'Our best
friends used to live in Columbus but have moved out', i.e. to
other suburbs or neighbouring towns. This man named Lima,
Ohio, 89 miles away. A third, a civil engineer, considered that
it took at least five years to make a friend. Questioned, it
appeared that in four years he and his wife had not reached the
point of inviting neighbours to an evening coffee party. Yet they
arranged a party for my wife and me: we noticed that the other
guests were relatives and friends from another town. Their
nearest close friends were in Dayton, Ohio (66 miles away).
The above statements are typical of many others made by
American families who were interviewed. They illustrate a
marked contrast in the way of life in the two countries. Every
American family has at least one big car, which can cover many

miles in a very short time on the wide straight American roads, with relatively little physical effort on the part of the driver(s), at low cost. A one-day outing to visit friends living 200 miles away on Lake Erie, i.e. 400 miles in the day, was not an unreasonable price to pay to retain a friendship of long standing. Increasing use is made of the internal airline system for the same purpose.[1] In England, such a trip would be unthinkable under present conditions although the rapidly increasing mobility of the nation is creating a different outlook amongst young people especially.

A lonely, middle-aged, American housewife, childless, wife of a garage foreman, to whom reference was made earlier was, perhaps, not as friendless as our description may have suggested. 'Most of the neighbourhood visiting round here is between young people who have children. They find friends this way,' she said. She meant real friends and not acquaintances. Her real friends, also, had been made when she was younger, and most of her visiting was with friends who lived in other parts of the city. Her visits appeared to be frequent.

Conscious, and sometimes very determined, efforts are made by Americans, especially the womenfolk, to keep in touch with friends through formal and informal organization. The Childhood Conservation League groups are referred to elsewhere. But briefly, these are informal groups formed by young mothers, ostensibly to help them with child care, which are frequently carried far beyond this period of need: we met women of 50, once members of the C.C.L., who still met as a group once a month in each other's homes. Others continued friendships made at church, when they were younger. For example, a university professor, aged 39 years, and his wife had maintained contact, over a period of ten years, with a group of a dozen families whom they got to know through the social activities associated with the church to which they all belonged at that time. The members of the group are now scattered over the various suburbs, open countryside and some have moved to

---

[1] During my second visit to the United States, as Visiting Professor at Louisiana State University, I more than once made an air trip to give a lecture on a university campus two to three hundred miles distant from Baton Rouge, Louisiana. This kind of journey is a routine experience in the United States.

nearby towns but the *wives* meet in one another's homes once a month for coffee and conversation. Occasional but infrequent *family* gatherings are organized, for instance a picnic in one of the state parks where a picnic shelter is reserved by the party. We encountered more than one group of middle-aged women who had met at least once a year since the days when, as youngsters, they were in the 'Camp-fire Girls' organization together. Whilst they did not now sleep around the camp-fire they managed some form of 'fire-raising' during their weekends together.

Whilst the American family moves more often from town to town and from subdivision to subdivision, as the economic status and needs of the family change, old friendships need not be, and indeed rarely are, discarded as would be the case in England. The high degree of mobility enjoyed by the American family makes possible a continuance of these close friendships between people separated by quite considerable distances. A few seek to make new close friends in their new neighbourhood but the majority, clearly, do not. On one subdivision four families had retained their membership of, and kept up their attendance at, the church in their previous neighbourhood and still belonged to church organizations as well as attending Sunday services. Some retained offices, for example as chairmen of various church committees, others continued to sing in the choir and some participated in social activities.

One family on a better-priced subdivision—charming people of working-class origin in a professional neighbourhood—said without malice but a little sadly, 'Our best friends are in West Side (a suburban district of the big city). Everybody up here is to themselves.' However, their two cars and no children made it unnecessary for this household to rely on new friends nearby. The wife visited her relatives and friends in town several times each week, and they in turn came out to parties which, in summer, were held on a patio well equipped with 'chaises longues' and deck chairs. In winter, parties were held in the basement, a real American party room with plastic-tiled floor suitable for dancing, pastel-blue painted walls and, at one end, a bar.

In both countries, some newcomers from a distance were met

who said that initially they had felt cut off from all their old close friends. Said one of them (husband 57 years, wife 55 years), 'Several (neighbours) may develop into close friends. John and Mary Jean next door are of the same age and are grandparents like ourselves.' Her husband interjected, 'and their mother lives with them too'. The wife continued '. . . and the Newtons across the street. . . . We had their key and took the papers in when they were on holiday'—this was said rather proudly. These two people felt the need for new friends and they had moved house often enough in their lives to know that it was sometimes difficult to make friends quickly. This last transfer of employment had taken them more than three hundred miles from their old home.

A young couple, in England, who also found themselves in a new house in a strange district expressed a similar need to make friends but at the time of our visit had made little headway. A feeling of frustration persisted throughout the interview. The husband, a commercial traveller (salesman), referred to 'a certain amount of "standoffishness" in the neighbours but this is typical of Bristol. Birmingham and London are different.' Another young couple, childless as yet, aged 28 and 30 years, echoed this assessment of Bristol people, but a little more tolerantly. The wife said, 'I found it very lonely when I first came here. Bristol people I found more reserved than I had been used to. People don't invite you to take part in activities.' This sentiment is frequently expressed in the correspondence columns of the local paper by newcomers to the Bristol district. Unfortunately for this young couple, the husband was perhaps too aggressive in his approaches whilst the wife was too backward; during the interview she echoed most of his statements but did so submissively or at least with little evidence of personal conviction.

One feature of the new life in a new house in a new district is often overlooked by people who have lived a long time in one home, namely that it takes a long time and a lot of hard work, on the part of the husband and wife, to turn a new house into a comfortable home. This is especially so if ready money is not plentiful, which is usually the case with families moving house. It is also very relevant if the new occupants are young and are in the process of bringing into the world, or bringing up, a young family. Present-day, 'do-it-yourself' processes and practices are not making the settling-in process any shorter; indeed it often lengthens it by persuading householders to tackle, sometimes quite intricate, jobs which a decade or so ago they would have left alone or called in the builder. Gardens have to be brought into a semblance of order as soon as possible, rooms have to be decorated, cupboards constructed and cabinets made. We lost count of the number of basements we were introduced to in America by proud do-it-yourself exponents. Plastic tiles laid to the floor, acoustic tiles fixed to the ceiling, hard-board panels nailed to the wall, shower-cabinets installed, the list of jobs was endless. England showed less variety and the emphasis was on woodwork—cupboards, shelves, etc.; an adequate provision of cupboards is usually provided at purchase in most American homes. Unfortunately, the Englishman has nothing comparable with the American basement wherein to demonstrate his ability with saw and chisel and, occasionally perhaps, to work off his ill-humour at the same time. He must display his skill, or his clumsiness, on the kitchen table, cool his enthusiasm in a draughty garage or, in summer, turn to gardening.

These household activities of newcomers take up a great deal of leisure time and sometimes leave little for friendly exchanges. The American couple with three young children who were building their own home (with help) recognized this and said quite frankly, 'Our closest friends are where we used to live. We had time (then) to make really close friends. For the first two years here we were too tired working and finishing the home', i.e. to give time to neighbouring activities. The young wife went farther, 'I like to stay at home so that my kids know that I am here'; with three children aged $7\frac{1}{2}$, 5 and $1\frac{1}{4}$ years of age, and a tight budget to work to, since they were building and furnishing the house out of income, the American equivalent for the English phrase 'gadding about' had no meaning for them.

Several American wives experienced difficulty in distinguishing between real friends and acquaintances. They could not see the point of the question. They had so many friends, they said.

Most of these women were in the 40 to 50 age-group and were involved in a great many out-of-home activities. One housewife insisted that all thirty members of her church circle were her close friends. This may well have been so because the family had retained their membership of a downtown church through three changes of residences over the last 19 years. Both she and her husband held offices in the church—she was 'polio captain', i.e. organized the periodic 'drive' for funds for the relief of polio victims. Quite clearly it depends on one's definition of 'close' as applied to friends. The following illustrates this difficulty of interpretation. One husband we interviewed maintained that 'We don't have any close friends here. My friends are all over Ohio.' Yet during the first part of our visit his wife was holding an animated conversation on the screened front porch with two neighbours who, judged by English standards, seemed to be fairly close friends. The wife later confirmed our judgment. The only *close* friends the husband recognized, however, were those linked with his two all-absorbing hobbies: coin-collecting, of which it transpired he was an acknowledged expert, and boating: 'When we go up to the Lake (Erie) we are all "buddies", but here I don't pay any attention to them.'

One wonders where exactly to place the friends referred to by our informant who knew most of the neighbours: she listed at least 12 by name for us. She said, 'We have become especially friendly with one family. . . . We do not exchange home visits. Our attitude is "live and let live" and not to get too close with neighbours.' Her husband must have felt that this sounded rather frigid and added, 'My wife and I are not much for visiting back and forth.'

Summarizing this chapter briefly, one could say that in England many of the newcomers would have liked to have made new friends in their new neighbourhood but, ironically, there were few avenues whereby this could come about. By contrast, in America, fewer newcomers sought to make close friends of their neighbours but the formal and informal occasions where stranger could meet stranger on a friendly footing were legion.

8

CHILDREN AND NEIGHBOURING

ENGLISH *housewives* 'get to know' their neighbours and American *homemakers* 'get acquainted' with them. Few English or American families had made friends, i.e. become close friends, with their neighbours through their children for the simple reason that, as we have shown in the last chapter, neighbours are rarely regarded as actual or potential friends. Many, however, had become friendly with their neighbours.

The young mother often gets to know her older neighbours better when she has some simple childish ailment to cope with. This kind of neighbourly action has already been referred to in more detail in Chapter 5. The needs for advice or help with the children led to introductions and, subsequently, to greater friendliness on both sides of the Atlantic, but other features pointed to contrasts in the way of life of the two groups of nationals. For instance, the straying of young children is a fear which was experienced from time to time by English, but seemingly at all times by American, mothers. It was mentioned several times in England on only one council estate which has been referred to already, where an open-plan layout has been adopted.

'When children are small they have to be watched all the time in the yard and it is more interesting to talk with an adult while keeping an eye on the children.' This is interesting as illustrating the development of neighbourly relations, but it could only be an American comment. In England, the builder of a new house does not usually expect to do more than mark the boundaries of the land on which it stands with posts and wire. The occupants soon solve the problem of keeping their own young children in, and their neighbours' children and dogs out, by erecting an adequate fence or planting a close, quick growing hedge of bushes. Side gates are then fixed to keep the children in the back garden, under mother's eye while she is about her work in the kitchen, and away from the traffic hazards and the possibility of straying if they are playing in the front garden: 'We work together with our neighbours. The next-door neighbour arranged his garden layout to suit ours. They levelled it and we erected a wall together', i.e. a boundary wall separating the two adjoining plots. The erection of common boundary fences in the early days of residence provides a useful excuse in neighbourly co-operation in England which is not available to Americans. Without co-operation between neighbours it can lead to serious friction.

The road outside the property is especially feared by all young American mothers who tend to regard every teenage driver of an automobile as a potential killer. On every sub-division there were references to this danger. These harassed mothers were shocked when we told them that the favourite play space for children on most new estates in England was the street, i.e. on the pavement (sidewalk) in front of the property. Partly for this reason, the cul-de-sac layout of estates which had only one entrance and exit was greatly appreciated by English parents with young children. In more than 12,000 miles of motoring in the United States neither my wife nor I met a single new subdivision where sidewalks were laid out. When we questioned the wisdom of this practice the reply given to us was invariably, 'We don't walk any more.' They could have added, 'It is cheaper', but no one did. Only two American families out of 120 expressed the view that new subdivisions should incorporate sidewalks in their layout.

In England, small children are encouraged to bring their playmates into the back garden to play and this makes for friendly intercourse between mothers of young children. The English walled or fenced garden, however, is not ideally suited to older children's more-boisterous games. In towns, these youngsters are expected to work off their energy in the nearest public park, and town dwellers moving out to a peripheral estate miss this amenity acutely. 'There's nothing for children to do', or 'There's nowhere for them to go', was a common cry we met. Many added that 'they' (meaning the local council) ought to provide a park or recreation ground for the children. In the meantime the youngsters play in the street, on and off the highway, in someone's garage way or on any piece of undeveloped land they can find.

The absence of boundary fences, and parental taboo on playing on the highway, means that American children are given a greater freedom to roam over the yards of their friends in neighbouring homes. This can be disconcerting to a foreigner who finds his quiet conversation with his host rudely (and I mean rudely) interrupted repeatedly by the youthful participants of a ball game being played in someone else's yard several houses away. The general absence of flower beds and the predominance of grass reduces the risk of damage but encourages the menace. In England, father's roses and mother's prize dahlias are special features of the garden which, quite early in their lives, children have to learn to avoid whilst at play. At times, these hazards may add zest to the game but a correctional discipline is at work all the time for most English children from the toddler stage onwards. This has not to be endured by American children who are not brought up to respect the privacy of the neighbour's yard in the same way.

There was some evidence that this freedom of access to one's property is not appreciated by all American householders and that frictions between neighbours sometimes occur. For instance 'Our early friendships were mostly made through the children, but some of the early disagreements were caused through the children. The children are now playing but the mothers are mad', i.e. angry. Another American, a homemaker, said that one of the reasons she liked her new home so much was that neighbours 'do not "gripe" if the children make a noise in the yard'. She had clearly had some experience of the other kind. But, in general, it appeared that the freedom with which children roam across yards in the United States is rarely resented by their owners and that neighbours are, on balance, brought together by these youthful activities.

Nevertheless, during the summer months children do make nuisances of themselves; this is true throughout the civilized world. But the American mother seems to exercise more tolerance and to have greater resources and more energy; and she exercises greater initiative. The American urge, and the talent, for organization shows itself even in the way mothers arrange their children's leisure. While seeking some shade in a state park some ten miles out of the city we once watched two mothers, three teenagers and six quite small children wriggle themselves out of one elderly station wagon. A couple of neighbours had come to the rescue on a hot sweltering day, scooped up the youngsters around and brought them out for a day's freedom in the country. Who provided the cases of lemonade and hampers of food we never learned but a happy noisy time was obviously enjoyed by all. Subsequently, we saw this operation repeated many times and learnt that this was the accepted practice in many neighbourhoods. On more than one occasion, our interviews with their parents were interrupted by a couple of boisterous juniors who burst in to ask if they could go with 'Mary Rose's mom' to 'Graceland', the local shopping centre. A glance through the window would show that half a dozen children and one mother were going off on the marketing (weekly shopping) expedition in the family car. In England, there are no state parks and fewer 'mums' have the use of a car and, if they had, the greater restraint between neighbours would probably have suppressed such a thought. An English housewife might take a couple of children, but half a dozen in the back of a Mini Minor . . . !

'There is nowhere to go . . . not even shops to look at. A shopping centre would be good. You get to know more people. . . . Even up to four or five streets away.' This English housewife was thinking of a group of a dozen small shops or less and not of an American neighbourhood shopping centre with its dozen or more supermarket-type shops retailing all kinds of food, household goods and equipment. Above all, she thought only in terms of walking since the family owned no car. The social satisfaction of a 'trip to the shops' is often overlooked; neighbours meet, words are exchanged and above all an excuse is provided for getting away from household chores and surroundings.

Baby-sitting by neighbours, so that parents can go out to a

show or some other outing together, is carried on in both countries. An English housewife who said that she and her husband were especially friendly with one neighbour, next door, explained that 'we exchange baby-sitting. We take them out in the car sometimes but,' she added rather quickly, 'we are not in and out of one another's houses.' Another included in her description of a good neighbour 'One who watches each other's children while the other goes out to the shops'. This is a very real service, for a visit to the shops, for the English housewife, is associated with some formality. During her walk she is on show to the neighbours. She sheds her houseclothes, dons her 'second best' outfit and the children are washed and 'made presentable'. Not so the American mother. If she is wearing shorts and a shirt when she discovers she needs something from the store, she jumps into the car and the only attention paid to propriety will be to powder her nose. Only if she makes a special visit 'down town' to the stores in the city centre will she 'dress up'. On other occasions, the children are bundled into the back of the car as they are and are regaled with ice cream or 'cokes' when they arrive at the destination: and they do not need their best clothes for this. The baby-sitter she will employ if she wishes to go out with her husband will most likely be the teenage daughter of one of her neighbours or friends who will be paid the appropriate local hourly rate for the job. This duty is rarely expected of neighbours gratis. The American homemaker has more pocket money than her English sister and is saved the inconvenience of having to perform a session of baby-sitting herself in return for a like duty. American teenage young ladies welcome the additions to their pocket money which come their way, from time to time, from the age of 13 years or so and continue through college.

Children provide the excuse for many 'cook-outs' and parties between neighbours on American subdivisions. Admittedly, the larger incomes and high standard of living make this easier but, at the same time, one must recognize that Americans enjoy parties more than English adults appear to do and that frequent parties are accepted as part of the ordinary way of life. On new subdivisions, peopled with predominantly young families, those without, or with grown-up, children tend to remain a little apart from the others. Mr. and Mrs. X. who were both approaching sixty years of age counted themselves fortunate to have made 'real friends of Mike and Winnie' their next-door neighbours who were their own age. They recognized that they were out of step, 'agewise', with their neighbours, and that, in the normal course of events, the chance of making friends was thereby lessened.

In England, after the age of 7 or 8, youngsters usually make their own way to school maybe with an older brother, sister or friend, to see they do not get into too much mischief. Below this age mothers expect to take them to the infants' or primary school. This may be not more than fifteen or twenty minutes' walk away, but to make the journey four times a day can be a burden, or at least an irritation, especially when there are other, pre-school-age, children in the family who have first to be dressed and taken along as well. Neighbours commonly help one another by performing this chaperon duty in turn. On the other hand, on a pleasant afternoon, several mothers will share the companionship which the journey together offers. Friendliness between neighbours results. Around any primary school gate on a sunny afternoon at, say, 3.30 p.m., a group of mothers will be found pleasantly chatting together and perhaps admiring, or envying, the handsome new pram of one of their number. The expensive basinette, an essential purchase for every young mother, is not met in America. Strollers or carry-cots for the back of the car, Yes. Prams, No.

By contrast, the American school child is normally taken to school by car until he or she reaches the age to own a bicycle. But a bicycle is only used until 14 or so, at which age I was credibly informed by several parents that 'no teenager would be caught dead on a bike'. (In fact, most parents are not greatly concerned by the reluctance to indulge in this form of healthy exercise since it relieves them of anxiety as to their children's safety on the busy roads: some may even encourage the disinclination to take exercise in this form.) Once the novelty of cycling has worn off he is once more taken to school by car. An American friend of ours, who had recent Scandinavian blood in his veins and still retained a healthy respect for the value of physical exercise, insisted that his son should walk the twenty minutes' journey to school whenever it was fine. Unfortunately for his high ideals, and perhaps fortunately from the child's point of view, one or other of the neighbours invariably 'took pity on the boy' as they were driving their own children to school. We were told that on an average he did not complete the journey once a week to school. For the journey home in the afternoon, we found that at every school there was a fleet of cars driven by mothers who were waiting for their offspring at the school gates.

Before English readers have time to pass comments on the 'softness' of American youth, we must hasten to remind them that the school is probably twice as far away, that there are few or no sidewalks, and that the American highway in the early morning or late afternoon is the last place to indulge in the 'quaint' English diversion of walking.

The need to take children to school each day is a very important factor in deciding parents with young children not to 'turn in' old cars when a new car is ordered but to keep it for mother's use. Many mothers co-operate in car pools for the transport of children to and from school. When the family owns only one car, mother drives father to work on one or two days a week so that she has the use of the car for school transport, shopping and various social purposes. (We met one or two families where the wife could only drive a car with a fully automatic gearbox, i.e. the new car, and father had to content himself with the old one on these occasions because only he could operate a gear lever.) When the oldest child reaches the age of 16 years, in most States, the problem is solved, for the child that is, since he is then old enough to get a licence.

American families enjoy several facilities non-existent in England, which tend to bring parents together through their children. The school and the parent–teachers' association are dealt with in another chapter. Another facility, family membership of the local, open-air swimming-pool, where a thousand or so youngsters and their parents may spend much of the sweltering summer day, is a very potent force in bringing neighbours together through their children. Weather, cost and the apparent inability to organize like the Americans, make this experience rare for English children. In England, parents gather on the sea's beaches with their children on special outings during summer weekends or the holiday month of August, when it is hoped the sun will be kind. The rest of the time children are mostly expected to amuse themselves.

Most of the households interviewed included children. Where they did not it was clear that fewer friends had been made amongst neighbours. Thus, in England, a young couple, both out to work, said, 'There are two groups of people, the established families and those who are just starting. We don't get much opportunity to get to know them. When we get home and have got the meal the evening is gone.' Thinking she had perhaps revealed too much of their private life the young wife hastened to add, 'But I like my privacy.' In America, one elderly couple had been in residence for more than a year but had not, so far, joined in a single local party. Their children were grown-up, married and living in other towns. The old folk's closest friends lived in other neighbourhoods and they spent much of their spare time away from their own home. Neighbourly 'cook-outs' did not draw them; they had little time for neighbouring and the wife had only been into the homes of the neighbours on each side. These two examples illustrate that in both countries, if you have no young children in the household, it is still possible to be alone and to live a life quite separate from your neighbours. In America, however, if you have young children it is next to impossible to keep apart from your neighbours unless you belong to one of the minority groups and are, for example, a member of the Roman Catholic community or, of course, coloured.

9

CHILDREN AND TEENAGERS: THEIR SCHOOLING AND SOCIAL ACTIVITIES

F ROM time to time, mention has been made of differences in the school system of the two countries and the bearing these have on neighbourly relations. This chapter attempts to bring together these features and to explain their effect on the day-to-day lives of newcomers on new estates and subdivisions. It does not attempt a comprehensive description of American education or, later in the chapter, of teenage activities.

To a visitor from England, the most important difference is that the American school *belongs* in a much greater degree to the parent and the family. The 'school board' which is elected by a local committee has absolute power over the running of the school. This is seen especially in its control of the school staff. The local board can 'hire and fire' the staff members at will. A nine-months' contract for assistant teachers is usual. The headmaster, or school superintendent, may be engaged for a longer period, but if he incurs the displeasure of the local board he can be relieved of his post without reference to any higher authority.

Cost of Schooling

The cost of the local school system is borne almost entirely out of local taxes.[1] (Taxes may be translated into English as

---

[1] In Worthington Incorporated District, where the three highest-cost subdivisions were located, the purchase price or erection cost of the homes, including the cost of the land, varied between $18,000 (£6,428) and $25,000 (£8,929). At the time of the survey, the local taxes of this incorporated district amounted to

district council 'rates', although this is not strictly true since trading profits and such useful items as automobile fines may help to support the local authority's general expenditure.) One locality may be tight-fisted and the next open-handed as regards education. One will gain an excellent reputation as a 'good school district' whilst the next may be considered indifferent in this respect. As we show elsewhere, many parents, especially middle-class professional families, with incomes of $8,000 (£2,857), annually, and upwards, were very largely influenced in their choice of residence by the high reputation of the local school system. This fact emerged repeatedly during the interviews.

Whilst school education in the United States is 'free', i.e. paid for from taxes, as in England, the total of out-of-pocket expenses for school clubs, personal equipment, travelling and incidental expenses of schoolchildren, which has to be found by parents, can be considerable. Costs soar when the child passes on to college where an outlay of $2,500 (£893), per annum, would not be regarded as remarkable and in some colleges is as much as $4,000 (£1,432). Families, middle-class and many working-class, which we interviewed, where there were school-age children, were clearly worried about the rising cost of education, and our question on family saving for the future very frequently included a reference to 'college education'. We found that most families had a savings fund for children's education. This worry as regards the cost of education we did not find in England where university education is achieved by a lower percentage of the total population, but substantial state grants make it possible for any young person who passes sufficiently highly in school certificate examinations to complete a course of university study once he has been accepted by the institute of higher education.

This higher family cost of educating youngsters may, of

$39.60 per thousand dollars of the tax valuation of the home. As an example, a house whose cost price was $25,000 (£8,299) was assessed at $10,000 (£3,571) taxable rates so that the actual local taxes paid were $400 (i.e. £143) per annum. In this locality the cost of building is relatively high and the taxes, especially the school tax, is also higher than in many comparable fringe districts to other cities.

course, explain in part why, compared with English parents, the American parent takes a far greater interest in the school and education generally. It touches his pocket directly. But, the burden appears to be accepted as part of the natural order by most parents and, paradoxically in this highly individualist country, whatever the cost, the American parent seems anxious to conform to the prevailing parent image. We received no adverse criticism of the system, the cost of participation in individual activities or indeed the total cost of putting a youngster through school and college. In fact, some parents seemed rather proud of the financial burdens they had assumed to this end: they clearly wanted us to appreciate the sacrifices they were making, or were prepared to make, at the same time bringing out how fortunate they were as individuals and as a nation to be able to afford such high expenditure.

Parent–Teachers' Association

Whether they wish to participate or not both father and mother are required to pay their annual subscription to the Parent–Teachers' Association. Disapproval expressed by teacher and class pupils corrects any backsliding on the part of parents, both as to subscription and attendance at the regular evening meetings of the Association. For example, the pupils may be given stars if their parents belong to the P.T.A.; these are withheld if they do not. Father may be strong willed enough or may have better excuses to give the parent–teachers' meeting a 'pass' fairly regularly, but mother is soon shown by junior that she is letting him down if she fails to put in an appearance regularly. In all honesty, one must admit that we found most fathers considered it a not unpleasant duty. The above comments are true for middle-class, but are less true for working-class, Americans. In 20 per cent of all American families interviewed parents belonged to the P.T.A. On one of the higher-priced subdivisions, where the proportion was 40 per cent (50 per cent of families with no school-age children living at home are excluded), the P.T.A. had clearly brought together residents living at opposite ends of a new subdivision, both at the regular formal meetings and at the more informal socials and drives for various school projects, of which there seemed to be a great number in some districts. On the lowest-cost, project, sub-division only one parent was a member of the P.T.A. out of 20 families.

By contrast, in only one English district were any parents members of a Parent–Teachers' Association. Here, on this one estate, three (out of 20) parents belonged but the proportion for the whole 120 English interviews was a mere 3 per cent. No resident had chosen his house because the neighbour-hood had a better school system. Furthermore, there was no evidence that parents felt the local school belonged to them in any special way. Had they disapproved of any school pro-cedure they could have taken little direct action, except to complain to the headmaster, the local county council repre-sentative or to write a letter to the correspondence columns of the local evening newspaper. 'Hiring' was a matter for the county education committee, which sat more than 30 miles away in the county town. 'Firing' of teachers is something almost unheard of in an English State-operated or State-aided school and an appointment can be regarded virtually as for life if the appointee so chooses.

The fact that in one of our survey areas a Parent–Teachers' Association pursued a very active existence showed that the apathy need not occur, even in England, and it was noted by one of our informants that 'newcomers are well to the fore in the W.I., P.T.A. . . .'

Childhood Conservation League

The sense that American schooling belongs and should belong to the *local* community, instead of a 'far-away' organization, is fostered in Americans from early childhood even before they actually attend the state school. Parents of children under five years of age voluntarily band themselves into C.C.L. (i.e. Childhood Conservation League) groups which may comprise ten or a dozen mothers of young children. The groups meet monthly, in different homes, and listen to speakers discourse on various aspects of rearing children. When no special speaker is present the meeting resolves itself into a discussion group.

The groups are affiliated through district organizations to an area, a 20-county association, which holds annual and seasonal conferences. Meetings are arranged by district and area administrations. Like the P.T.A., the C.C.L. groups appear to be, more especially, middle-class activities. None were met on our three lowest-cost subdivisions.[1] On the two highest-priced subdivisions, mothers who were members of C.C.L. groups comprised 10 and 20 per cent of the whole interview sample, respectively.

It was noticeable that mothers—it is peculiarly a mothers' organization—referred to '*my* C.C.L. circle'. The emphasis on the personal pronoun reflected a strong sense of belonging and instances were met where the C.C.L. grouping continued as a social grouping long after the children had passed through the infant stage. One such group had been in being for 15 years during which time it had changed itself into, mainly, a hospital fund-raising group which helped and sponsored charitable drives of all kinds. Our respondent was rather vague as to what actually took place at the meetings: 'We get together once a month in each other's homes. We talk. We sew. We plan for the next drive': i.e. collection for benevolent purposes. This was not very explicit. Nevertheless, it was noteworthy that a group of young mothers which had got together so long ago, and now were 45 or 50 years of age, still derived enjoyment from meetings which now, as perhaps always, seemed primarily for personal social satisfaction. A second unusual feature was that in spite of American mobility as to residence the group had continued in being for so long.

No similar local voluntary organization exists in England. The official child-welfare clinic comes nearest to it, but is much more highly organized by, and is officially the responsibility of, the county council. A doctor and nurse are in attendance at the centre on 'clinic day' to give expert practical advice on babies' welfare as well as to talk on more general topics of interest to mothers with young children. The medical staff and the accommodation are provided by the county council and parents are put to no expense. In some districts, mothers serve

[1] Subsequently, during my stay in Louisiana, I learnt that the organization was unknown in the Deep South.

on local child-welfare committees which arrange social efforts, but there is little voluntary effort or informality about the child-welfare clinic system in England.

Nursery Schools

In general, English children start at (State) schools at 5, and American children at 6, years of age. There are a few private and fewer statutory nursery schools in England although private ones appear to be increasing in number. In America, if two or three mothers with pre-school-age youngsters think that a nursery school would be desirable, and there is none available locally, somebody does something pretty quickly and there is one. The procedure which we met in several places is always the same and follows, roughly, this pattern. Half a dozen mothers meet over a cup of coffee in one home and form a 'nursery school group'; one offers her basement as a classroom, another says she knows a woman who used to teach. Within a few days the teacher is engaged by the group and the nursery school is in being. Each mother pays her share of the total costs; sometimes she shares, in turn, the job of instruction, on a basis of, say, one morning every two weeks. Parents in one group we met were contributing half a dollar (i.e. 3s. 6d.) a day for three days' school per week. This could not happen in England for a number of reasons, the most important being that everybody would wait for somebody else to start the thing off. Contributory reasons are that there are no basements and only in old Victorian houses are there rooms large enough to serve as classroom for six or ten lively youngsters. In a modern home, what English housewife would turn her 'best room' over as a school room? Trained teachers need to be adequately paid and there are few English mothers of young children who could find the necessary money. Finally, and very important, is transport. None of the American children would be walked to the nursery school by his mother, as would be the case in England. A car pool would be formed by those mothers who had the use of a car so that all children would be taken to, and brought from, school. The teacher might live the other side of the town but she would certainly have a car at her disposal if she made a practice of taking teaching assignments. This is not an exercise in baby-minding. At one of our interviews a little girl of 5, who had just returned from her second lesson at a nursery school, obligingly filled in the details as to what happened on our tape-recorder as follows: 'We pasted . . . (a long pause) . . . we had some books on . . . we played with the blocks . . . coloured blocks. Then we had juice and crackers . . . (another long pause). And we played games and sang songs. Sometimes they go for walks.' The last was added brightly. She was clearly looking forward to further delightful new experiences.

Since our survey was completed, 'toddlers' groups' have been formed on two of the English council estates. A small subscription is made by the parent to the local community association which appoints a qualified person to instruct the pre-school-age children, for five days each week, either for the morning or for the afternoon sessions. The buildings where the groups meet are approved by the public health authority. The essential difference between these and the American nursery groups is that the parents do not organize the affair themselves and, in fact, take no part in the day-to-day running. Mother is free to take herself off shopping, attend to her housework without interruption or even to take a job.

Extra-Curricular Activities

Extra-curricular activities play an important part in the everyday life of the average American teenager. In a good English secondary school there are camera clubs, nature-study societies and the like, but no English school child could hope to compete with the following list of activities engaged in by one American 16-year-old girl:

She was a member of the school Y-Teens. This is a girls' teenage organization, found in many schools, which raises money by every conceivable device for charitable purposes, such as to help physically-handicapped children, for whom American state welfare provision is slender by English standards. Domestic articles are made and sold, concerts arranged and dinners sponsored. This last activity needs explanation for the English reader. As mentioned on another page, Americans appear ever ready to assemble for a party and what more worthy effort than a meal put on in the school hall by a class of 16–17-year-olds to which one's own daughter or niece belongs? The evening programme will be organized entirely by the teenagers. Parents provide the food as gifts to charity, and all parents, uncles, aunts and friends are dragooned into buying tickets at a dollar-twenty (8s. 6d.) or a dollar-fifty (10s. 8d.) to attend a noisy, friendly, free-and-easy meal at 6–6.30 p.m., served in the school dining-hall on the cafeteria principle, which allows friends to sit with friends and neighbours with neighbours. There is little excuse for neighbours with teenage children, after having experienced one of these gatherings, continuing to address each other formally as Mr. or Mrs. this or that. Christian names are the order of the day 'in no time at all' to use another commonly-used expression.

But to return to our 16-year-old. Because she was going to be a school teacher she had joined the school Future Teachers' Association. By English standards the school was a large one, and the F.T.A. group had between 50 and 60 members. The group receive regular talks from members of the staff on elementary teaching theory and practice, and the girls do a certain amount of class supervision, including sharing some class duties with the teachers. Some members belong to the F.T.A. for as long as four years before leaving school for college, depending on the age at which they had decided to take up school teaching as a career.

Like most other youngsters of her age she was a member of the school Girls' Athletic Association, which had its own set of officers drawn from the different levels of the school. She played hockey, basket-ball, baseball and the like. During the summer vacation she was employed, and received payment, as a life-guard and instructor at the swimming-pool. Most schools which possess their own playing fields operate a 'summer programme', as it is called, for the first six weeks of the summer vacation when instruction is given, to those who enrol for classes in swimming, tennis, physical training, handicraft, etc. The total area on which the Worthington School stands slightly exceeds 80 acres including the built-over area, recreational area, athletic fields, picnic area and the swimming pool and its associated sunbathing lawns.[1] She was a member of the cheer-leading club which held meetings and practices and, of course, attended most school team events where 'touch-line' encouragement was deemed useful and appropriate.

Another regular school duty came as member of the school office reception staff. For this unpaid privilege she arrived at school several mornings a week at 8 a.m. to help the secretarial staff with their work, and to interview children and parents calling before the school opening at 9 a.m.

To fill any other spare moments of the week she was a member of the Methodist Church and shared its social and religious activities. She belonged to a Methodist Youth Club which held a regular social meeting each Friday evening.

At home she had a study bedroom to herself (she was an only child) where she listened to her radio. There was a second television set in the basement where, if she so desired, she would watch any special show with her friends without interfering with the normal activity of the household. On one bedroom wall a large 'bulletin board' displayed details of her various activities and engagements. The above programme suggests that she needed these reminders. Her father remarked, only half jocularly, 'If you want to talk with her you have to make an appointment at breakfast'; this meal was eaten at the bar separating the living-room from the kitchen. The whole family had streamlined their lives to be able to get necessary duties, like eating, carried through as efficiently and smoothly as possible, because mother held a part-time job which meant she left home with the others every morning. Need one add that our teenager can drive a car? In fact, her father wished that he could afford to run a third car to cut down the taxi work he and his wife have to do to enable his daughter to meet her engagements. No doubt her boy friends help out on occasions.

This young woman of 16 was no exception, for most boys and girls of this age whom we met seemed just as 'intense' in their zest for life. For my wife and me the most significant fact arising from this teenager's programme was the earliness and

---

[1] A newly-built English secondary school which enjoyed 15 acres of playing field, garden area, etc., would be considered to be lavishly endowed.

the thoroughness of the training in leadership and sense of community responsibility. In fact, this training begins much earlier than 16. This was indicated by the words of a 13-year-old girl we met in another home. She was a member of the Girls' Athletic Association at the school which meant that she made use of the various school athletic recreation facilities. It appeared that she stayed behind after school to play, according to weather and season, baseball, basket-ball, badminton, volley-ball and to use the swimming pool. The organization of this association was in the hands of scholars, with one member of the staff present at meetings as adviser. She was also a member of the Students' Council which is elected annually, as she said, to 'assist in running the school, solving student problems, and helping student–teacher relationships': these actual words came spontaneously from the lips of a youngster just 13 years of age. The Council comprised two representatives from each class with two teachers attending as 'sponsors'. General and specific subjects are discussed at regular meetings but an important part of the Council's function is to organize social activities, such as dances, and to sell school supplies during 'noon time' to gather funds for school projects and activities. She was an active member of the school Y-Teen Group described above.

Besides these school activities she belonged to a 4-H Group formed by one of the parents living on the subdivision. This group of a dozen or so youngsters met once a week for instruction in domestic science in a church schoolroom, under the supervision of another mother, a graduate in the subject, who gave her services free to this voluntary organization.

The child came from a very ordinary home. Her father was earning between $5,000 and $7,000 (£1,786 and £2,500) as an instrument technician in a factory. He expressed himself happy for his daughter to be so well occupied but transport had been difficult since they had, until recently, possessed only one car. (No American parent allows his daughter on the streets after dark.) The home furnishings were 'homely' and the parents 'working-class' by English standards, but there was no indication that they regarded their younger daughter as being very different from their older who was attending the State University, or from any other youngster of similar age. For

them, this was the normal pattern of activity for a girl of 12 or
13 years. But 'transport of teenagers is a major problem', they
repeated. It appeared that neighbours helped when their own
children needed transport from a school dinner or other social
or educational activity. The child, herself, saw the lack of a
second car as a factor acting as a brake on her freedom of
'expression' as she termed it. She clearly felt no sense of inferiority and it was not so much that they could not *afford* a second
car which worried her, but the fact of not having one 'restricted'
her participation in school and family activities, and prevented
the parents leading as full a life as their neighbours or as they
would have liked to do themselves. (An older daughter had
recently learnt to drive and the position was eased now that
they had two elderly cars—a six-year-old Ford and a nine-year-
old Chevrolet.)

The extra-curricular activities of American high school boys
appear just as numerous and time-consuming as those of the
girls. For them, the Hi-Y, a benevolent organization, roughly
paralleled the girls' Y-Teen groups. They share the control of,
and participation in, the activities of the Athletic Association.
The thoroughness of American organization was brought out
by a lad of 19 years who was present during our interview with
his parents. He had graduated from high school and was completing his first year as a student at university. At high school,
he said that, in addition to sharing the activities of the type
mentioned above, he had been particularly successful in various
school 'projects'. For example, he had belonged to the school
speech group (debating society), the members of which wrote
and presented papers on various set topics. The best debaters,
selected by school competition, proceeded to the area schools'
competition: thence the winners entered the State speech competition and so on to national level.

A second school project with which he had been concerned
was in science. This he shared with a school friend. The two
chose as a thesis project 'The preparation of paper'. In the
course of their researches, they visited paper mills and libraries
and, finally, succeeded in developing a method of manufactur-
ing hand-made paper, on sheets of which they eventually wrote
their description. Having been selected to represent the school,

the two lads successfully demonstrated their method of manufacture at an area contest from which they proceeded, once again, to a State competition. Having achieved an 'Excellent' award at this level, the two had reluctantly to withdraw because the next stage, at national level, would have meant a stay in New York which would have been more expensive than the family felt it could afford. This all took place in his last year before going to college and at his own expense. His father made some financial contribution but much of the money was obtained by the lad himself through out-of-school employment, during school holidays, at the aircraft factory where his father was employed. There is a moral here somewhere for English schools and English parents.

It has frequently been said in these pages, that the Worthington Incorporated District enjoyed a good school system, but English readers should not assume that it was in any way extraordinary in its provision of out-of-school activities or that these teenagers are in any way an exception. They were, in fact, quite ordinary specimens of their generation. As for the school, we learnt of another where there were forty-nine extramural activities from which pupils could choose those which interested them. Some schools wisely restrict the choice to four or five at any one time but there is an immensely wide range of activities for all ages. In this school there was a course of ballroom dancing which most youngsters in their 5th and 6th grades[1] enjoyed during the winter months. Many have clubs to teach automobile driving and car maintenance. Even the best English school's out-of-hours programme is pathetically slender by comparison.

It is true that English schools are smaller but the school roll of the Worthington School whose activities are described above comprises all grades from 5- to 18-year-olds. The total roll was 3,250, but the high-school grades, i.e. grades 9 to 12, roughly 15 years to 18 years, included some 700 boys and girls. This is 175 or so in each year, a figure which does not greatly exceed

---

[1] A high school graduate is a student who has successfully completed the twelve yearly school grades, which run from the first at the age of 6 years in the Primary school, through the Junior High, to the twelfth grade in the last year at the Senior High school.

that in some of the larger English grammar and secondary schools. No! the difference is in the interpretation by staff and children as to what is meant by the word 'education' and in the enthusiasm shown by both sides, but particularly by the pupils.

Social Activities for Children and Teenagers

The survey has brought out the contrast in the greater number of social activities associated with American churches and schools, compared with those in England, but we have so far ignored more-broadly-based activities, such as Boy Scouts, Girl Guides and youth organizations generally. Table 16 makes it quite clear that participation by American far exceeds that by English children and teenagers.

No English youngsters belonged to more than one organization, and they had no church or school clubs or activities to attend either. In all, about a quarter of all the boys and one-sixth of all the girls were members of Scouts, Guides, Youth Clubs, etc. In America, nearly three-quarters of all the boys and well over three-quarters of all the girls belonged to at least one activity of this kind.

The 66 American membership units included some duplication. Table 16 shows that, in America, one-third of all the boys, and one-quarter of all the girls, between the ages of 8 and 16 years, belonged to two or more organizations; three girls, i.e. between 8 and 9 per cent, belonged to four social activities; again we must repeat that this takes no account of church or extra-curricular school clubs and societies in which we have seen a high proportion of youngsters participate. It is noticeable from Table 17 that this multiple membership was confined almost exclusively to the three higher-priced subdivisions; in other words, this feature of the social activities of youngsters comes from middle-class, and not from working-class families: the latter are content to belong to one activity. Further, girls seemed better joiners of social activities than boys: all the 16 girls on the three better-priced subdivisions belonged to at least one social organization compared with 17 (out of 22), i.e. 77 per cent, of the boys; indeed, more than half of these girls belonged to two or more. It would seem that the habit of belonging to clubs and social organizations, seen so strongly amongst women on the higher-priced subdivisions, is laid in childhood.

TABLE 16

Children and Teenagers' Organizations

	Total
England	
Boy Scouts, Boys' Brigades, Youth Club	9
Girl Guides, Brownies, Youth Club	4
	—
Membership units	13
Number of participants	9 boys (out of 32)
	4 girls (out of 25)
U.S.A.	—
Little League	6
Boy Scouts and Cub Scouts	23
Girl Scouts and Brownies	15
Campfire Girls and Bluebirds	14
4-H Groups	8
	—
Membership units	66
	—
Number of participants	25 boys (out of 35)
	29 girls (out of 35)

English readers may wish to know a little more of the other organizations listed in Table 16. More important, those who are concerned with youth activities in England may wonder where the leaders are found to control such a high proportion of the total youth population. The answer to the second point is that American parents are persuaded, induced or desire to take a much more active part in training their offspring in social activities. By contrast, English parents, accustomed for generations to leave this to the parson and the young lady from the 'big house', merely shrug their shoulders whilst complaining that 'there's not enough for the children to do'.

The Little League organization, which teaches young boys the rudiments of baseball, basket-ball, wrestling, tennis and the like, illustrates the above. This is a national organization with subsidiary bodies controlling Little League activities in each of

TABLE 17

Child and Youth Activities

	England			United States		
	Total	Estate		Total	Subdivision	
		3 higher-priced	*3 lower-priced*		*3 higher-priced*	*3 lower-priced*
Boys between 8 and 16 years	32	11	21	35	13	22
Engaged in one or more organized activity(ies),	9	2	7	25	8	17
in 2 activities	—	—	—	9	1	8
in 3 activities	—	—	—	3	—	3
Girls between 8 and 16 years	25	13	12	35	19	16
Engaged in one or more organized activity(ies)	4	1	3	29	13	16
in 2 activities	—	—	—	3	—	3
in 3 activities	—	—	—	3	—	3
in 4 activities	—	—	—	3	—	3

the 50 states. In every neighbourhood there is a local club which is administered by parents who have boys between the ages of 8 and 12 years. Most children participate and father is expected by his children to play his part in coaching. The actual training may take place in the local park, in the school grounds or on a waste patch of ground not yet built over. We noticed that, on a fine summer evening, the number of parents some-times seemed to exceed the number of children; it appeared to us that the practice pitch provided a convenient focal point for neighbouring—especially between fathers.

This parental training in games is extra to the school organized games periods which follow the ordinary school instruction. Parents are expected to take an interest in school sports as well. At the Worthington school, which was attended by children from the three higher-priced subdivisions, the parents had formed a 'Booster Club' or Supporters' Club which organized social activities to raise funds to improve the facilities, sport and social, for the school children. Some of the funds so raised were put at the disposal of the Little League. The rest were used to improve the dressing-rooms, playing fields and canteen facilities belonging to the school. Substantial sums were raised and spent annually by the Booster Club. This was the story as told to us by a founder member of the organizing committee. Some few years earlier, half a dozen people met in a private home one evening to consider the provision of athletic facilities for children in the locality. They set up a committee which included a local doctor, bank manager and a professional basket-ball coach. The school staff is not represented on the management committee but the junior high year of 14-year-olds is because they are responsible for collecting the one-dollar subscription from all and sundry. After every basket-ball and football game a canteen is run by a committee of adults; 500–600 children are fed by a group of six or seven adult couples. The feeding part of the proceedings is followed by a social entertainment provided by the youngsters. Occasional special events are held, such as the ox roast the previous year which had raised $2,200 (£720).

The school co-operates, for example, by providing premises, and for some Booster Club projects it matches the Club's financial contribution. Projects to date have included the provision of nine baseball diamonds, two electric scoreboards (just like the University's, I was told proudly), tennis courts, etc.

In England, amateur and professional adult cricket and football clubs are similarly helped by their Supporters' Clubs but the idea has not been applied to youth organizations. This is regrettable since a great deal of potential money, leadership and, above all, parental support and goodwill remain untapped.

The principle of parental participation is also found in the Girl Scout and Boy Scout movements. For instance, the youngest boys, from 8 years of age, are formed into small groups of six or eight or so Cub Scouts and are put in charge of one or more 'den mothers'. These last are parents who serve for a period of six weeks to three months after which they hand over direction of the group to other parents. The Cub Scouts gather weekly at the home of the den mother on duty. At the age of 11 or 12 Cub Scouts are transferred to a Boy Scout troop to which fathers are expected to serve as assistants. Each troop will have half a dozen parents carrying out various duties under a scoutmaster, who is regarded as the expert and who instructs the parents in the responsibilities expected of them. These include serving as leaders or assistants for organized games, handicraft activities, camp instruction, fund-raising campaigns, etc. Even after the age of 15 some parents continue in the organization leading the older lads in special projects designed to keep the group together.

Mothers share similar duties in the girls' organizations, such as the Girl Scouts and the Camp-fire Girls and the Bluebirds. Whilst we were in the United States, our hostess disappeared one weekend to join her old group of Camp-fire Girls on a two-day outing with six others on a cabin cruiser on Lake Erie. The previous year they had gathered at the weekend, lakeside cottage of another of their number. We were told that these activities had taken place annually for thirty years and the members travelled to their reunions from many states. This is clear evidence of the effectiveness of the training given in the original youth organization.

The 4-H club organization is nationally organized and is financially sponsored by each state. Little propaganda is carried out to promote 4-H clubs; it isn't needed for its effectiveness is sufficient advertisement. Clubs come into being in the following manner. One or two parents feel that a club for their children would be desirable, so a general invitation is passed around the neighbourhood and parents meet for coffee in one of the homes or, if there are too many, in the schoolroom. A committee is set up and a general programme decided on. Some fathers want a woodworking group for their teenage boys. In a farming area they may ask for a farm group. A group of mothers feel that their daughters are of an age to profit from instruction in

cookery or dress-making. Groups within the club are formed
to cater for these interests. They then call on the 4-H club
District Agent, who is employed by the State and works with
the Agricultural Extension Service of the State University. He
comes along and addresses the group. The local community
has to find its own leader, usually one of the parents; junior
leaders are soon found from amongst the older children. Neither
leaders nor instructors are paid. 'You are usually in it because
your child is in it,' said one mother who was instructing a
dressmaking and a cookery group. She held a degree in home
economics from the State University.

Members pay $1.50 (10s.) a year and provide all the equip-
ment, tools and materials needed for instruction. They meet
literally anywhere: in the church hall, schoolroom or somebody's basement room. In a woodworking group which met on
school premises, we discovered that both the leader and the
children provided their own tools; it was explained that the
youngsters will need woodworking tools when they become
adult, so why should not the parents provide them now when
the child could be taught how to use them properly. One
wonders what would happen in England if members of the local
education authority handicraft class were told that they were
expected to provide themselves with a set of woodworking
tools for class use.

In the State of Ohio there are 10,000 voluntary leaders and
instructors and 85,000 members of 4-H clubs registered with the
Extension Service. Local clubs are affiliated in a county federation. (The county is an area roughly comparable with an
English Rural District.) County and State competitions are
held from time to time. Every State maintains a number of
permanent hutted camps, staffed with paid wardens and
domestic staff during the summer periods, which are taken over
for varying periods by different County Federations of 4-H
clubs: the County Federation provides the organization whilst
their members are in residence. All the discipline and much of
the day-to-day running of the camp are assumed by a couple
of dozen junior leaders, known as counsellors, elected from the two
hundred or so youngsters in residence. These counsellors help to
carry out the educational, athletic and recreational programmes

of the camp programme with remarkable efficiency, as we saw at first hand. They meet each day to discuss details of discipline, the following day's programme and all matters relating to the smooth running of the camps. In one home we visited the parents regretted that we should not be able to meet their daughter who was away at camp: she had attended three that summer, namely the Girl Scouts, Camp-fire Girls and her 4-H club group. The summer vacation is long—at least three months —and parents as well as the children welcome these breaks. A copy of the programme of one camp is given in Appendix C.

The important features of the programmes described above are the sense of responsibility instilled in the young, and imposed on parents, the training in leadership and the cultivation of an awareness that, if a social need arises, it is the duty of the ordinary citizen to set about filling it, using local resources wherever possible. In most cases this means that the individual has to put forth some money, time and energy himself. English parents we interviewed on new estates, council and private-enterprise alike, were full of moans and grumbles that there were too few opportunities for the young to fill in their spare time. From house-owners came the following: 'Our son (a teenage apprentice) goes nowhere to meet anyone. We need a Youth Club.' 'Children must meet and play with others. It's not right that they should be kept in the limitations of the house.' From two council tenants came similar expressions: 'We want something for the teenagers and the courting couples. We want a community centre.' 'This is a completely new place and clubs are needed.' No American parent passed this kind of remark to us. Many English mothers took their tiny children to the swings in the park, or for walks along the river, but only one father, he had been a professional footballer, appeared to give up any significant portion of his leisure time to training his children; he played football and cricket with them and took them boating on the river. The remainder seemed to play with the baby, help with the washing up and potter about the garden. They expected the older children to look after themselves and grumbled that there were too few facilities for them to do so effectively. When the English interviews were taken I, myself, found this attitude unremarkable. It was only when

I came to study the records again, having in the meantime met, at first hand, the enthusiasm displayed by American parents, that I began to notice the attitude of my own countrymen.

The sharing by American parents of responsibility for the inspiration and organization of activities for children and young people, in and out of school and church, must have a profound effect on neighbouring and neighbourhood friendliness, especially on new subdivisions, as parents are brought together by a common interest in their children. So must the absence of interest shown by English parents.

IO

THE CHURCH

THE Churches and the pattern of churchgoing in the two countries exhibit a number of striking contrasts. It has been estimated that 75–80 per cent of all American compared with 10–12 per cent of all British people attend Church. These figures cannot be considered to possess any great statistical accuracy since they depend so much on how you define a churchgoer, his frequency of attendance at devotional services, his financial contributions and so on. But it can be accepted that in America a minority only of the population does not acknowledge some kind of Church affiliation, whereas, in England, it is the minority which does so. Only eight Americans out of our sample of 120, i.e. 7 per cent, stated that they did not attend Church and the majority of the rest were quick to point to membership of one or other social or semi-social Church activity as well. The abstainers were quite definite as to their non-churchgoing: for example, 'The Church is in walking distance but we haven't walked it.'

By contrast, in England, it appeared most unlikely that more than a dozen families, i.e. 10 per cent, attended Church services regularly (Table 18). This is a rough estimate since so many English adults tried to avoid giving a direct answer to our question concerning Church attendance: many tried to divert attention by saying that their children went to Sunday School every week. A minority were more honest: 'We used to be strong churchgoers until we came here, but since we have been here we have stopped going.' Then, in an effort to excuse themselves, 'Nobody called. . . . The children do go to Sunday School, though.' Or, 'We used to go to St. John's Church but

146

TABLE 18

Attendance at Church Services and Social Activities
(persons participating in at least one activity
as per cent of the whole sample)

	U.S.A.	England
Attended Church services:		
Husband⎫		
Wife ⎭	93	10 (probably less)
Belonged to Church club or social activity		
Husband⎫	19	2
Wife ⎭	33	7

we don't go now. Mind you, I like Church.' One or two explained that they were so busy: for example one husband told us, 'I used to go to Church every Sunday when I was in Bristol but I have to work every Sunday now to cope with the increased rent, etc.'

In no English home was there evidence that any Church had made a real effort to get the newcomer and his family to attend Church services or activities. The situation in the United States is entirely different. There, the Churches are continually reaching out for new members. The Welcome Wagon hostess, whose activities are referred to again in the next chapter, enquires the Church affiliation of all new families *immediately* they move into the new house. The information, including the newcomer's telephone number, is passed on immediately to the appropriate Church, even if no strong Church affiliation in the old neighbourhood is apparent. Each of the larger Churches maintains a Church office, manned by a paid and/or voluntary clerical staff, which opens from 9 a.m. or so each weekday. A responsible Church member is detailed to invite the newcomer to come to Church and to join the 'Church community'. If members of the newly-arrived family attend a Church service, a welcoming letter is sent to them and someone else telephones to say how pleased they were to meet them; later, the minister calls. This general pattern of welcoming newcomers is followed by most

Churches in the United States. One Church we visited placed printed cards in all pews inviting a visitor to put an 'X' against any of the Church activities listed in which he was particularly interested. This led to a follow-up enquiry and a welcome from an officer of the activity specified by the newcomer.

The majority of newcomers, especially those who have moved from a distant town or village, experience some loneliness and the American system catches them just when they are most vulnerable. As far as Church attendance is concerned, as one minister put it, 'If they had been backsliding in their old parish, the hand of welcome is held out just when they are likely to need it.' One household spoke of the 'warm feeling' they experienced when they went along to the Church of the same denomination they had attended in Indiana. The people were so similar and the service was the same they said: 'We felt at home immediately.' For this man and his wife there had been no break in the continuity of their churchgoing.

The Protestant Churches of the United States, and it is of these we write since Ohio has been a Protestant stronghold for over a century, are 'aggressively outgoing', as one parson described them.[1] It seems an apt description. No such attitude was met in England: there the Churches of the neighbourhoods surveyed appeared to be mainly neutral in their outlook to newcomers. The children had been welcomed to Sunday School but not one family had been invited, welcomed or encouraged to join the Church or its activities by a *personal* visit from a Church officer or member. It is true that one Church had pushed some leaflets through some of the doors.

In most English Free Churches, devotional services, mainly for adults although children do attend, are held on Sunday mornings and evenings. In Anglican Churches services are held on Sundays and throughout the week, the number varying with the ecclesiastical calendar. Questioned, an American minister explained that throughout the United States fifty years ago, 'When I was a boy it was unthinkable that you should not attend morning and evening services and, if you were young, a Sunday afternoon meeting as well.' A very very few sects still

[1] Six American and five English families were met where one or both parents were members of the Roman Catholic Church.

insist on this pattern of Church attendance on Sundays. But, between 1920 and 1940, the larger Churches—the Methodists, Baptists, etc.—gradually dropped the evening services: now, children's services are held on Sunday mornings and not afternoons as is almost invariably the case in England.

Over the last twenty years or so Church attendance in the United States as a whole has increased noticeably. One Church in one of our higher-priced neighbourhoods had 520 members ten years ago. It now has more than 1,400 members and its roll is increasing at the rate of 150 new members each year: much of this has been due to the influx of newcomers into the district. Similar trends of membership increase were reported by other Churches. The important point, however, is that increases on this scale were not shown in the English neighbourhoods. Here, in this Church also, ordinary devotional services are no longer held on Sunday evenings: 'Most Churches have gone over to multiple services on Sunday mornings.' To use the words of a minister, 'We are not bound by the traditions of the past. They (the members) choose what is most convenient for them.' This was a sly dig at the more rigid interpretation, as he understood it, of religious observance by the Church of England. He added that Americans would raise their hands in horror if they were expected to feel an obligation to attend Church two or three times on Sunday; 'I don't think our people would stand for it,' he said.

American Church buildings tend to be smaller than those of English Churches and most will seat only 250 or so. This explains the need for duplication of Sunday morning services as American Church congregations have increased. In most, services will be held at 9 and about 10.30 a.m. for adults in the main Church building, or sanctuary, while children meet downstairs in the basement or in a separate schoolroom building.

Almost all American Churches have well-equipped schoolrooms. Children's services and children's education are a basic part of Church life in the United States, and in each Church thousands of dollars are provided annually by members for this purpose. Several factors operate to make this desirable and possible. We have seen that American parents are vitally interested in the education of their children—more so than English parents: for most this includes religious education. Religious freedom is fundamental to the constitution of the United States and no religious education or instruction is allowed in any state school. Therefore, in order that a child should receive a grounding in, or even a smattering of, the Christian faith, he must attend classes arranged by one or other of the Churches. The Church authorities in the United States have recognized that in providing this sought-after instruction they can 'get right into the family'; as it was explained to us, they have something to offer the family which cannot be obtained anywhere else. This 'right of entry' to the home used to be held by English village parsons but was lost when the Church relinquished its role as the main provider of rural education in the village school. This was forecast time without number at meetings held to protest against the 'reorganization' of village education into primary and secondary in England under the 1944 Education Act. Only the parson felt it important.

A sizeable American Church will have a set of classrooms equipped as well as the best day-school, with school furniture, play equipment for the younger children, story books of all kinds, cine and still projectors, record players and television. It will employ at least one full-time, paid, education adviser who has been specially trained for religious education at one of the degree-giving colleges of the denomination. I am reminded of this by a Church magazine, before me as I write, which records beneath the portrait of an alert-looking young woman, the following: 'Coming in August to direct our work in religious education, Miss Gloria Lanbhumer brings to this Church a splendid collegiate training in religious education and experience in methods in Churches in Morristown, Tenn., and Chicago. She will be working with Rev. Clark and Mrs. Richards and our Church school staff.'

In this Church at 9 a.m. each Sunday morning, at the same time as an ordinary service for adults is held in the sanctuary, the following classes meet: Pre-nursery (1 class), Nursery (1 class), Pre-school (1 class), Primary (3 classes), Junior (2 classes), Seventh Grade (3 classes), Eighth Grade (3 classes), Ninth–Twelfth Grades (2 classes), older Youth (1 class), Merry Weds (1 class) which is described later. During the 10.30 a.m. service two school classes are also held, Pre-nursery and Nursery, to enable parents to worship in the sanctuary while their very young children are kept suitably occupied elsewhere. This was a summer programme, when attendances tend to be smaller, and in the fall the children's 10.30 a.m. programme is extended to include classes for older children for whom there is insufficient room in the 9 a.m. class.

Services at this and most other Churches do not exceed one hour and, I quote from the Church magazine, 'The 30-minute interval between services and Church school sessions beginning July 5th provides time for a hospitality hour in the dining-room. Friendship Service Class will be held from 10 to 10.25. This increased interval between services is your opportunity to become better acquainted. Join us then. The longer interval between services should lesson congestion in our parking lot.' From observation, we could add that attendance at the earlier service made it possible for the family to get away in time to proceed to one of the state parks and enjoy a 'cook-out' picnic at midday, instead of returning, as in England, to a traditional Sunday dinner of roast joint and two veg.

'To become better acquainted.' This expression one meets on every hand in connection with secular and religious activities in the United States. Everyone everywhere seems to want to become better acquainted. Following, or perhaps leading, the trend the Churches emphasize their social activities and, to quote one minister, 'Some people may be in Church three times in the week—if not on Sunday.' The belief that it is the purpose or the function of each Church to provide a comprehensive pattern of social activities is held by few Churches in England. This is reflected in the fact that out of about 240 English adults only 20 membership units of social activities (men and women) were recorded in our survey (Table 18): in fact, only 2 per cent of all male and 7 per cent of all female adults interviewed were members of Church social activities in England. In America the corresponding figure was 82 units for men and women. It is noteworthy that higher-priced subdivisions showed a high proportion of adults who were Church members and attended Church social activities.

What reasons lie behind the highly-developed social activity associated with Churches in the United States? Firstly, Americans

seem to possess to a stronger degree a sense of 'togetherness'
which impels them to gather in groups for friendly conversational interchanges. Secondly, they quite clearly enjoy a sense
of *belonging* as one of a family to clubs and organizations of all
kinds: this feeling is used by Church officers who give to as
many members as possible responsibility for specific duties. Jobs
may not be actually manufactured or duplicated but the number of officers sometimes appeared excessive (to an Englishman). Thirdly, to provide the range of services which the
Churches considered necessary or desirable needs a great deal
of money which would be difficult to obtain via the offertory
box; activities or responsibilities which help to increase the
Church income are vital. Fourthly, few Churches in the United
States claim to exist solely to provide facilities for devotion.
Church activity is not something apart but is, for many families,
an integral part of their daily life. Fifthly, and this came from
several ministers in various forms, 'You haven't to talk philo-
sophy, politics or religion or anything very deep. Members are
offered a better-looking carrot.' Sixthly, and finally, we were
told often that many middle-class Americans are members of
the Church and its activities because it is the fashion to do so.
As one parson put it, 'People look down their nose at people
who do not take part in Church projects. The penalty for with-
drawing is isolation from the community.'

Taking these six reasons in order, it was clear from our own
observations and experience that Americans love to gather with
their friends in groups, especially, as we have already noted, if
the excuse for doing so includes eating in some form or other.
'The symbol of feeding is closely associated with Church activity.
The sure thing to make something go over when it is on the
rocks is to have a dinner,' said one Church officer, an academic
member of the State University. Church-sponsored dinners and
suppers are features of the programmes of almost all Churches
in the United States. Members of the public are invited and
the gatherings commonly include Church members and their
friends from near and far. A group of members, perhaps a
Church 'circle', or maybe a teenage club, will cook and serve
the meal. It may be a chicken barbecue, a fish-fry or a pancake
supper. The eating may be followed by a sale of work or

a jumble sale. At other times it will be a lecture, discussion or just social entertainment. A Church may hold a 'home-coming' evening when old friends are invited to come back for a dinner and a meeting. The proceedings may be open to the whole Church or to one section. For instance, the Men's Club of the Presbyterian Church at Worthington meets five times during the winter months; and between 60 and 70 at a time will sit down to, say, a chicken supper; on another occasion, known as 'Father and Son Night', fathers prepare a meal for their sons. At the last meeting of this kind, 85 fathers shared this duty, the proceedings being followed by the screening of a movie film of a football game.[1]

The Worthington Presbyterian Church has a Young People's Group which meets every Sunday evening at 6.30 and is attended by an average of twenty-five 16-year-olds. A panel or quiz entertainment will be followed by a movie. Alternatively, an outside speaker, a doctor, lawyer or public official, may be invited to speak of his work; refreshments are organized by the young people. Out-door 'cook-outs' are arranged for summer Sunday evenings. Every Church has its dining-room, which may be a place specially set apart for this purpose; alternatively, it could be the schoolroom, or simply the basement room under the sanctuary, which has a well-equipped modern canteen kitchen at one end. The nearby Methodist Church has a similar organization for young people, known as a 'Teen Stop', which meets in the club-room of the Church which is fully equipped with billiards table, table tennis, etc. On Friday or Saturday evenings there will be a social or dancing. The record player and tape recorder are well used and a regular rota is maintained for staffing the canteen for the supply of coffee and hot snacks. Every Sunday evening a brief devotional service is held in the club-room; this is followed by a discussion or talk and general 'socializing'—there is no English equivalent for this expressive Americanizing of the English language: 'unplanned recreation' is the nearest one can get to a translation. In this case, we were told it included young people sitting round the stove talking while they were 'stashing the food'.

[1] The total number of families officially listed by this Church as members is six hundred.

One shudders to think of the reaction of the average English minister who discovered such goings-on in the Church Hall on Sunday evening.[1] In England, not one teenager was a member of a Church group. The average English parson and his Church officers dislike too great an emphasis on social activities associated with Church life. They do so on two grounds. Firstly, they feel there is a very real danger of social activity taking precedence over devotion, which they regard as the prime function of the Church. Some consider it the sole function. Secondly, especially in rural areas, the Church is concerned that the local community should act and think as a community. They feel, quite sincerely, that too much sectional social activity tends to divide a community into separate camps, the Anglican group, Baptist group and so on; they fear that there would be too few people to support all activities satisfactorily. The weight of the Church is therefore usually directed towards supporting village or district organizations and activities for the local community as a whole. The reply to this must be that, in the United States, neighbourhood activities like the Parent-Teacher's Association, the Red Cross, etc., are supported just as, and as we have seen frequently more, strongly than in England. The American Churches, acting as institutions, encourage this participation in general community action as well, and their members, maybe because they are such 'good joiners', comply.

The sense of belonging to the American Church, referred to above, is encouraged at all times in many ways but perhaps the most noticeable, to an Englishman, is in the, apparent, proliferation of official duties and responsibilities. Details of the committee structure of several Churches in the neighbourhood of the American subdivisions studied are reproduced in the Appendix. Here in the text we shall refer mainly to one, a quite small Church, where beside the Official Board of Trustees there were Commissions (Committees) for Education, Membership, Finance, Missions, Social Relations; there were committees for Music, Building, Pastoral Relations and the Parsonage building. Other groups included the Women's Society for Christian

---

[1] A youth club attached to an English Baptist Church was recently forbidden even to play dominoes: they moved across the road to a room in the local public house.

Service, two choirs, Mothers' Club, Men's Club, Play School committee. Each of these groups or committees has its chairman, vice-chairman, secretary and treasurer. And this is a small Church of 140 families. If we take one of these groups, say the *Women's Society for Christian Service*, we find that it has a president, who serves as chairman and represents the group at general Church organization committees; the vice-president takes charge of the programme carried through each season by the Society; there is a secretary; the treasurer handles $1,200 (£428) a year; a membership chairman sends cards for meetings and makes calls for new members of the Church and she has a committee as well; the *Christian Social Relations Group* raises funds for various charities and sponsors a study course; the *Spiritual Life Group* arranges devotions; the *Youth Division* helps with the youth work; finally the *Local Activities Committee* sponsors social efforts like the church suppers. This small Church has only two women's 'circles'; groups of 20 to 30 women who meet in one another's homes once a month for social purposes: a larger Church may have upwards of ten or a dozen. There are two choirs, a junior and a senior, with a paid director. The Church has a Cub Scouts pack and the older boys belong to the Scout group of another Church nearby. The *Mothers' Club* meets monthly to sponsor projects to help the Sunday School, by raising money, and by providing volunteers for recruiting drives to enrol newcomers in the Sunday School. The *Men's Club* meets periodically for discussions and socials of various kinds; it contributes a great deal of voluntary help to keep the Church building in repair; for instance, crews of men were working in turn painting the parsonage while we were interviewing the parson. The men of the Church run a baseball team. A *Play-School Committee* organizes a nursery school on three mornings a week for thirty 3- to 5-year-olds. A number of yearly events, such as camps for young people during the summer, complete the picture of the social activities of this lively Church community. Each club and association has its quota of officers and there can be few members of the Church who are not officers of one group or another. This sense of active participation in, and direction of, the activities of the Church cannot fail to instil a feeling of belonging and of ownership so that we found most individuals spoke of *my* Church and families referred to *our* Church; never did we hear of *the* Church.

The effort to ensure that Church activities are related to the everyday life of its members has been seen in the emphasis given to eating and dancing or general conversations on Church premises. It is also reflected in the subject and the mode of presentation of the Sunday sermons and the titles of discussions. Religion is shown to be a part of everyday affairs. Sermons deal with how to conquer worry, to master fear or to get along with your neighbour. The interest of the congregation is captured by drawing attention to an everyday problem which is then examined in the light of Bible teaching. The subjects for sermons for two consecutive weeks in one Church magazine read as follows: 'David and Goliath: Brain Will Tell' and 'Daniel: Lions for Room-mates'.

To the same end, Church organization is so arranged that there are activities for family and for groups of all ages and sexes. Where an English Church would run a single women's group, e.g. Mothers' Union, an American Church will have several. Thus Worthington Methodist Church has a Women's Society of Christian Service with several hundred members which concentrates on 'devotion, and serving the aims of the wider Christian Church and sponsors special efforts of Christian endeavour'. It has also a group called the 'Merry Weds' which comprises some 200 members, 80 or 90 of whom meet for divine worship on Sunday mornings. These are all young people with children in primary and junior high school grades who attend morning Sunday school in the schoolroom at the same time as their parents meet in the sanctuary or another hall. Another group of younger parents, 'The Searchers', meet one evening in the week for devotional exercise described as 'questing'. The lists of Church committees contained in the Appendix demonstrate the special needs and interests which are met in these Churches.

The cost of providing the scale of services indicated is, by English standards, fantastically high. The annual budget of the small Church above is of the order of $15,000 (£5,357): this is met, primarily, by about a hundred 'pledges', each pledge averaging $120 (£43) a year. The total number of families is 140. About a half of the total expenditure goes in salaries and fees, the minister's stipend being $5,000 (£1,785) with a rent-free parsonage provided. A larger, Methodist Church, on an adjacent subdivision, needed an average *weekly* income of $1,530 (£546), approximately $80,000 (£28,571) per annum; pledges amounted to $64,000 (£22,857) of this. A still larger, Presbyterian Church with 1,400 members, about 600 families, had an annual budget of $180,000 (£64,286). Each of these two larger Churches had to meet the salaries of two ministers, an education adviser and paid clerical staff for the Church office. The salary for a senior minister in a large Church may be $7,500 (£2,679) a year, which is of the same order as that of a senior school teacher.

These relatively large sums are raised mainly by 'pledged' contributions from members, and in some Churches, although none of those referred to here, a new member must covenant on joining the Church. The principle of tithing is strongly advocated by the clergy of the United States, some of whom urge their members to give 10 per cent of their salary to Church and other charitable funds. One Church we studied urged its members to set aside 3 per cent of their salary towards maintenance of the Church and its benevolent funds, 3 per cent to the Church building fund and 4 per cent to the Red Cross, United Appeal and other worthwhile regional, state and national benevolent projects. The ministers, as individuals, are expected to set the pace in a pledge campaign and the amount of their contributions is well advertised amongst the congregation. Many ordinary people nevertheless appear to need some persuasion, applied in various ways, to put up their fair share of running the Church. The most successful method is to employ a professional fund-raising organization either to train the officers of the Church or, for special projects, to employ them directly as fund-raisers when they take a percentage of the sum raised. Using local resources, one Church raised $14,000 (£5,000) in one year for its special building fund. They called in the experts from a fund-raising firm the following year and collected $75,000 (£26,786). In this campaign it was made known that the minister had pledged one per cent of the campaign's goal from his own salary of $7,200 (£2,571).

The Churches of the United States have 'studied how to

motivate givers'. 'We don't send amateurs to do the fund-raising. We train our officers to organize the campaigns for pledge-making.' These two statements came from ministers of different Churches. In operation, a local committee is formed from the officers of the Church, chosen for their knowledge of, or ability to assess, the financial position of other members. The committee breaks up into parties of two which visit each member family in turn, describe the financial commitments of the Church organization and make 'suggestive askings' of the member. Americans pride themselves on their business ability—which they all like to think they individually possess. Most of them are interested in statistics—although we found some were rather less proficient in their use than they, themselves, believed. 'Bigger and better', if not 'Bigger must be better', is an expression everyone thinks he understands: in other words he is already conditioned to receive the trained manipulation of the Church representatives. He is told and accepts the challenge that the Church must grow in order to be healthy and that its finances must be soundly based to do so: his pledge is made and income-tax remission is sought from the appropriate authority. Whilst these negotiations are proceeding and the fund-raising campaign moves onwards, every individual member is made aware of the needs of the Church and accepts his responsibility for shouldering some of the financial burden. At the same time, he absorbs some of the sense of urgency which is seen to fire its officers.

The total sum pledged invariably falls short of the total needed and a variety of money-raising devices, known as projects, are resorted to. These are not left to haphazard organization. For instance, one of our large Churches had divided its 'parish' into 27 different zones with a deacon or zone chairman for each area. In all, over a hundred men are sent out during the year. (Where would the average English Church find a hundred men for this job?) To make sure that backsliding is kept to a minimum and contributions and pledges to a maximum, one hundred men are given an active job to do in the Church organization. They *have* to attend Church meetings to be able to do the job. As officers, it would be noticed if they began to backslide. Women are no less zealous. There is no shortage of volunteers for collection duties. 'People pile up credits for themselves in this way—or think they do,' said one parson, in a cynical (or was it mischievous?) moment. It was not made clear whether he felt that his parishioners believed they were piling up credits in the eyes of God or their neighbours. We did not ask. Probably he meant both.

The most common method of raising money for projects is the familiar one of organizing a meal followed by an entertainment. One such supper, which my wife and I attended, was held in the basement schoolroom. All the food had been donated by Church members and was prepared by a committee of ladies and served by a band of teenagers. The tickets were $1.50 (half a guinea) apiece. An excellent meal was followed by an entertaining talk by a visiting minister, a professional speaker who was paid a fee by a commercial firm of termite exterminators. My wife, who had been warned by our host that there would be a 'commercial' during the proceedings, was horrified to hear a parson extolling the virtues of his 'friends' the directors of the exterminator firm, who sat on the platform with him. He advised any of the audience to get in touch with them at the end of the talk if they suffered from termites. This announcement followed immediately on the singing of a hymn. We both found the situation a little incongruous, to say the least, but had to admit that the reverend speaker, so sponsored, provided interesting, worthwhile 'entertainment'. I fear that the message of the termite exterminator stayed with us longer than that of the parson—maybe because of the novelty of its presentation. Our friends saw nothing amiss in the programme. More unusual means are frequently adopted. The following innocent device, the travelling basket, appeared quite ingenious. A basket of fruit is donated by a member who takes it to a friend on a list provided and asks her to accept it and place a dollar (i.e. seven shillings) in the basket. The next week the recipient fills the basket with fresh fruit and with the dollar passes it to the next one on the list, and so on.

The 'better-looking carrot' to which the minister referred is not exactly a cheap article but, judged by the increasing membership of most Churches in the United States, it is a very good-looking one when an ordinary professional family is prepared to pledge anything up to $500 (i.e. £179) a year for the benefit of nibbling it. The extraction is regarded as fairly painless mainly because the individuals are made to feel that they are one of a big family and because the Church has something everyday and practical to offer them, namely all the facilities of a good club with special activities for father, mother and the children. An American household can stay out of the club and explain to others that they are not 'joiners' but only a minority choose to do so and these usually have some other, more absorbing activity, in which they indulge. It is rare to find both husband and wife in middle-class communities abstaining entirely from Church affiliation. Put at its lowest, on the one hand regard for the opinion their neighbours hold of them would be too strong and, on the other, Church organisers are very, very persuasive in their dealings with newcomers and backsliders. But, the real success of the Church in the United States seems to derive from its direction. I quote from a subsequent letter from one of the ministers we met there, 'the basic justification and a real part of the motivation comes from the theological understanding of a "gathered" rather than an "institutional" Church. There is an urgent necessity, theologically, to "gather all men unto Christ", which is still the root stock of all the social activity of the Church although it is covered over with much underbrush.' The Church leaders we met were good 'gatherers' judged by attendance at the great range of activities their Churches had promoted.

What use does the average American household make of this wealth of social activity, as distinct from attendance at religious services, which has grown up around the practice of religion in the Churches of the United States? We found that 19 per cent of the husbands and 33 per cent of the wives belonged to one or more Church social activity (Table 18). The breakdown of these proportions over the different subdivisions is interesting. Relatively few of the men on the three lowest-priced subdivisions shared this Church social activity and 15 of the 19 per cent male participation came from the three highest-priced subdivisions. Female participation was higher, but even here 23 of 33 per cent housewives came from the three highest-priced subdivisions. The effective proportions for the three highest-priced subdivisions are therefore 30 and 46 per cent participation for men and women, respectively. These figures indicate that, notwithstanding the elaborate pattern of religious and quasi-social activity associated with the Churches of the United States, in total a minority only of American families play active parts in their social life especially on low-cost subdivisions.

After this description of the comprehensiveness of the social activities associated with American Churches anything one can say of those of the English Church community must appear an anticlimax. In *English Rural Life*[1] I have given a chapter to the consideration of the place of Church and Chapel in the way of life of rural peoples. Here I shall merely repeat that of the 120 families interviewed in England less than 10 per cent ever attended Church at all: two husbands and eight wives belonged to Church activities: five of the eight housewives were members of the same group, the Young Wives Group of the Methodist Church on one estate.

This chapter did not set out to describe, comprehensively, the Churches of the United States or to contrast in detail the Churches of the two countries. We have picked out for description only those activities which appear to us to have a bearing on neighbouring and the neighbourliness of subdivisions and estates in the two countries. It is clear, however, from the foregoing pages, that, compared with Britain, in America a greater number of people know a great number of people and that this is due in no small measure to the way in which the Churches have succeeded in making the practice of religion a part of everyday life. The meals, socials and discussions inevitably bring adults closer together. The flourishing youth groups make sure that youngsters have opportunities to get to know one another. The benevolent 'drives' and collecting devices like the travelling basket provide reasons, or excuses, for women to call on one another in their homes. The committee structure of the Churches brings groups of people together regularly, often weekly, and, again, frequently in one another's homes. This they appear to welcome since Americans are trained from early youth to be 'clubable', with the result that, in middle-class neighbourhoods, at least, the non-conforming family is regarded as a little odd

[1] H. E. Bracey, *English Rural Life* (1958), Chapter 12.

and is grouped with Roman Catholics, i.e. as being different.
In one fairly long road on one of the higher-priced subdivisions
it was literally so: so many Methodist families lived in it that it
had been nicknamed 'Methodist Row'.

II

ADULT SOCIAL ORGANIZATIONS

IN all branches of each sphere of social activity, recreational, athletic or benevolent, we found that American participation was overwhelmingly greater than English participation. Strict comparisons are difficult since it is impossible to separate the social from the benevolent in such activities as Rotary Clubs, masonic orders or hospital circles, which American middle-class society seems to proliferate. Nevertheless, it will become abundantly clear in the following paragraphs that English husbands and wives are unenterprising stay-at-homes compared with their American counterparts.

Men's Social Organizations

Seventeen per cent of all English adult males could claim that they were members of a social club—a works club, community centre or an ex-Servicemen's club—the membership being distributed fairly evenly over the six interview groups; some admitted that their attendance was irregular and infrequent. In addition, one was a freemason (Table 19). Against these figures, 14 per cent male adult Americans were members of a social club, 7 per cent were members of luncheon clubs (Rotary, Lions, Kiwanas), 17 per cent were active in masonic orders (including Shriners and the Grotto) and four were associated with friendly-society social activities. In both countries, membership of ex-Servicemen's (Veterans') organizations was insignificant: 'I dropped out of the American Legion Club—I found it a waste of time and money. I joined like everybody did after the war.'

Summing up the position in the two countries as regards social clubs and activities, 40 per cent of all American compared with 17 per cent of all English male householders belonged to at least one social activity of the types listed in Table 19.

Approximately one-fifth of all American male householders attended the meetings of a professional society appropriate to their occupation, compared with only one Englishman who did so: he attended regularly because he was an official. These figures illustrate a major difference. The Englishman regards his professional association as an administrative machine designed to look after its members' professional interests, salary, conditions of work and so on. Meetings are for business, and any social activity more often takes place, informally, over a pint in the pub before or after the business proceedings. By contrast, the American is at all times ready to be educated. He is quite ready to listen to a specialist lecture after the business has been completed and he will expect some feeding provision, not necessarily to include alcoholic drink, in the same place at the same time.

In the United States, most enterprising business and many professional men, especially salesmen, get themselves elected to luncheon clubs or masonic orders if they can afford it. But there are exceptions. The following came from one young family man who had rejected this practice: 'Americans I know who belong to clubs feel that somewhere along the line the club will benefit them materially and get them a better job or more money.' He added, 'If I can't make it on my own, I won't. If the boss doesn't recognize me then I'll get a job somewhere else.' This young man had worked his way through college, supporting a wife and child, with long hours working during the evening and weekends at all kinds of manual tasks. 'You can't get a job nowadays without a degree or a diploma,' he explained. His skill and application were earning him promotion without his having to participate in social activities to which he was not greatly inclined and for which, in any case, he would have found it difficult to find the time or the money since he had yet to complete the fitting of the house he had built largely with his own labour.

The opposite, and more usual, point of view was held by the

TABLE 19

Men's Organizations and Activities (excluding Church)
(persons participating as per cent of the whole sample)

	U.S.A.	England
Social		
Social Clubs (incl. works clubs, country clubs, community centres, etc.)	14	17
Fraternities (incl. college and masonic)	17	1
Luncheon Clubs (Rotary, Lions, Kiwanas, etc.)	7	
Persons belonging to *at least one* social activity	40	17
Athletic		
Golf	4	1
Bowling	4	—
Sports Club (incl. tennis, cricket, football, baseball, yachting, archery)	11	9
Persons belonging to *at least one* athletic activity	17	9
Professional Society		
including Trade Union	18	1

older professional men, one of whom replied to our query as follows: 'Masonic organization? Of course! Most of my friends and relatives are masons. Masonry is strong amongst Protestant people. It moved in with the New Englanders (i.e. into the Middle West) who set up Churches here in 1804 and masonic lodges soon after.' This professional man, it seems, attended masonic meetings two or three times a year but visited with friends made there much more frequently. A neighbour gave four reasons why he and others of his friends joined masonic orders. He put first, self-advancement in business. Secondly, the habit of membership was handed down in his family. Thirdly, he said, 'You may have a friend who is a pretty good sort of a guy and you find that he is a mason and gets certain benefits. So you think why shouldn't you share them.' Finally, masonry is respected by the general public as the *top* organization, socially: 'Our lodge is the oldest lodge this side of the Allegheny Mountains.' We could add that it is highly likely that the absence in the United States of the welfare state health and welfare provisions, found in many European countries, has compelled Americans to 'invest' in masonic orders and friendly societies, in order to secure the benefits an Englishman receives from the State in return for the money he pays each week in contributions (dues).

There is some evidence that the fraternal orders in America are losing much of the appeal they held in the 1920's. The Moose and the Elk lodges are said to be having a hard time to keep enthusiasm going amongst their members and a high proportion of their membership is maintained because of insurance and other advantages. But, whilst the male lodges have been, in general, declining, the feminine auxiliaries have been thriving. Four of our American housewives were members of the Eastern Star masonic group. Three belonged to the 'Daughters of America' and three the 'Daughters of the Republic'. Three of their daughters had been elected to the juvenile masonic order known as 'Job's Daughters', to belong to which a youngster must be the daughter or grand-daughter of a freemason. At the junior meetings, which are held twice a month, talks, usually with a religious basis, are followed by general social activities, conversation, games and refreshments. Money-raising efforts are organized to give a purpose to the group, to provide club facilities or to further some charitable object.

Many masonic orders promote a great deal of social activity on behalf of various benevolent activities. One of the higher orders of masonry, the Shrine, specializes on fund-raising for a programme of building and maintaining hospitals and homes for crippled children. Their week-long annual junketing in a selected holiday centre, like Las Vegas, makes the headlines in the press from coast to coast. Some masonic chapters gain a reputation for attracting athletes as members. One of our informants, a member of the Grotto, was a keen bowler. His branch ran twelve bowling teams (indoor skittles or ten-pin bowling) with some 70 or so participants and rented one of the big commercial alleys, with thirty lanes, for one evening each week.

Luncheon or dinner clubs operate much as Rotary or Soroptomist groups in England. For example, members of the Lion's Club meet twice a month at 6.30 p.m., say. A substantial meal is followed by a brief business meeting and 'then we socialize', according to a member.

One luncheon club, the Deganas, especially interested us: we were told that it was typical of many others. This, primarily social, club had a sporting basis. Its total membership was some 700. A weekly luncheon gathering was held at a large hotel at which up to a hundred members sat down to a meal, which cost four to six dollars, to which a sportsman of outstanding reputation was invited as guest for the day. 'Most are business men but I'm an hourly wage man. Its more difficult for me, but I make it as many times as I can—usually three or four times a year.'

Whilst it is true that many American householders belonged to formal organizations of this kind there were seven who shared the view of one of their number, the head of a university department. 'I am not a joiner. We both work intensively at our jobs: then we are jealous of our free time in the evening'; he was speaking, also, for his wife. But this professional man was actively engaged in the social life of the Church and the University as well as in bringing up a very lively family. Had we been in his shoes we also should have found difficulty in finding time for further social activities: the social and academic life of the average university, alone, can take up a great deal of 'free' time. We hesitate to use the word 'leisure' for few academics appeared to have any—in the English sense. Most of their time was 'committed'. Most of the husbands interviewed by us who did not belong to formal secular organizations were involved in Church activities of one kind or another.

None of the English husbands had experienced the kind of intensive social activity to which Americans are exposed in childhood from the time when they join their first 4-H club, Scouts, Church group or school social activity. A few English-men had belonged to clubs when they lived in town. 'I used to attend Marden's Social Club (a works club) twice a week. But I haven't been since we came out here.' For the majority of fathers, 'My club is my family', summed up their feelings. Nevertheless, some English husbands would have welcomed machinery for getting together with their new neighbours had such existed locally. 'People are not community minded round

here.' 'There doesn't seem to be much social life for the over-
thirties.' In the United States, had they wanted to, both of
these newcomers would have found organizations ready to
welcome them, or if not would have set about doing something
about it.

TABLE 20

Women's Organizations and Activities—Excluding Church
(persons participating as per cent of the whole sample)

	U.S.A.	England
Social		
Social Clubs (incl. Women's Clubs, Welcome Wagon, Women's Institute, Townswomen's Guild)	24	14
Fraternities (incl. college and masonic)	19	—
Bridge Circles	15	—
Sports Clubs (various)	3	1
Parent–Teachers' Association	12	3
Childhood Conservation League	5	—
Persons belonging to at least one social activity	45	17

Women's Social Organizations

In England, the most important, and in most neighbourhoods
the only, secular social organizations for women are the
Women's Institutes, in more rural areas, and the Townswomen's
Guilds, in more urban ones. Fourteen per cent of all English
women were members of one or other of these two (Table 20).
But, since neither of these groups was present in the neighbourhoods where 40 interviews were made, this proportion can
be raised to 22 per cent for the neighbourhoods where the
organization was available.

American housewives had greater choice and almost one in
two belonged to some formal or semi-formal social activity
(Table 20). In Worthington, where the three highest-priced
subdivisions were situated, there was the Women's Club,
roughly comparable with the English Townswomen's Guild,
which operated an Acquaintance Group, as well as the Wel-

come Wagon.[1] These two organizations claimed 11 out of the eligible 60 housewives (18 per cent). On these same three subdivisions were to be found six of the seven women who attended college sorority meetings regularly and six who belonged to old scholars' groups from the schools from which they had graduated. The average participation on the three lowest-cost subdivisions was six out of 20 compared with 12 out of 20 on each of the three highest-cost subdivisions.

For English readers it should be explained that college closed student groups, operating to a semi-masonic formula, observe national affiliations. College fraternities (male) and sororities (female) expect membership to be retained after the student has left college. All the big city centres through the United States have local 'chapters' of the parent fraternities and sororities. Thus, one of our housewives, a woman of 31 years with two children, still attended her sorority meeting one evening every month: this was held at the home of one of the members, where refreshment, music and conversation were enjoyed. The register of the local chapter held one hundred or so names and it was said that 35 members could be regarded as active and regular in their attendance.

It is noteworthy that membership of the social organizations referred to above was almost entirely confined to the three better-class subdivisions and scarcely appears on the low-cost ones. At this point one is tempted to say that there is not much difference between English council-house tenants and the occupants of the low-cost American houses as regards membership of social organizations. Yet this is not true of less formally-organized social activities. It is not true of the informal bridge circles and groups, which American women, especially, form from amongst their friends and acquaintances and to which 15 per cent of all our housewives belonged. These groups have no formal rules or membership rolls although sufficient formality is observed to ensure a hostess and a meeting place from week to

---

[1] The Welcome Wagon organization is sponsored by the State, local town council, Churches and voluntary social organizations. A Welcome Wagon 'hostess' calls on newcomers with a welcome from the Governor of the State, an invitation from the Churches and gifts from the local tradesmen such as a quart of milk, voucher for a free 'hair-do', a token for a suit to be cleaned or an invitation to a meal 'on the house' at the local restaurant.

week, in the homes of the members in turn. Bridge clubs, then, are found at all social levels: they meet with varying frequency although rarely less than once a week. Sometimes they are husband and wife affairs and take place in the evening, but, usually, a number of women whose children are old enough to be at school meet at, say, 11.00 a.m. and play through lunch until the mid-afternoon. The hostess for the day in whose home the meeting is being held will prepare the midday meal, from contributions of the members supplemented from her own refrigerator. The bridge circle may comprise members of a single high-school graduating class which has kept together for 10 or 20 years. It may have derived from the P.T.A., Women's Club or Church circle.

Membership of parent–teachers' associations, to which reference is made elsewhere, was found on all subdivisions, but with a concentration on two where 40 per cent of all families belonged. The all-over proportion was 25 per cent compared with 3 per cent for the English estates. The activities of the C.C.L. groups, referred to in Table 20, are also described elsewhere.

No English housewife was active in a charitable (collecting) society; the welfare of hospital patients, crippled children and the blind are sufficiently well looked after by the State, although there are voluntary bodies which provide supplementary benefits or operate agency arrangements for certain statutory services. In general, it is true to say, that supplementary voluntary help for the sick and unfortunate in Great Britain may occasionally be desirable, but is only in exceptional cases absolutely necessary. In the United States well-organized propaganda by various pressure groups has made statutory welfare almost a 'dirty' word; well-intentioned women have plenty of scope to exercise their charitable inclinations, as well-to-do women have done through the ages. A high proportion of American middle- and working-class homemakers are very well-to-do compared with the unfortunates who are unemployed or suffer prolonged sickness in that rich country. Ten per cent of American housewives took part in collections or 'drives' for charitable organizations which rejoiced in the names of 'Wings', 'Twigs', 'Joy League', 'Beavers' Guild' or were known, simply, as the Hospital Guild, etc.

The British public has the impression, obtained from over-enthusiastic news reporting, that all or most American women spend their days rushing out to parties and clubs. The figures in Table 20 show that a great many do belong to regular social clubs and gatherings. Several women were able to list by name six or seven formal organizations to which they belonged, omitting all the informal coffee parties and Church activities. For example, a woman of 26 years, with two children aged five years, belonged to the following: 'Mothers of Twins Club, South-gate Masons, Swan Club, Joy League', and two other social organizations as well. But 30 per cent of all homemakers belonged to no secular club or activity. One of these, a college teacher, said, 'You've either got to have your house or your club —not both.' Speaking for her husband, she added, 'Some people are joiners but he is not. He has his friends but with his work he would not be at home at all (if he joined clubs as well).' They both belonged to the P.T.A. for the sake of their two little girls, but that was all. We met one or two, but no more, university professors who expressed similar sentiments.

American wives have so many organizations and activities to choose from that they can be selective, and rejective if need be. For example, another young mother, with children aged 2 and 4 years, said, 'I fought shy of the Childhood Conservation League. Most of the women have been in the coffee groups and I thought I'd be happier out of it.' This was a charming and rather serious young woman who gained more satisfaction from the college sorority groups she attended every month and from the select Columbus Symphony Group which also met monthly in one of the larger homes. (Attendance at these functions was of the order of 50 or 60 so that a really large home was needed; a commercial caterer was usually engaged.)

Some women, in both countries, seem to find bringing up small children a full-time, or at least a fully satisfying, job and they show little real interest in women's social activities, even where it would have been possible for them to attend, for example in the evening when father could take over baby-minding duties. 'I would like to join when the baby is older. You get to know people like that', came from an English mother whose first baby was only 10 months old. Her day was happily filled and she wanted no more at present.

Men's Athletic Activity

Seventeen per cent of all American, compared with 9 per cent of all English male householders, belonged to some form of athletic club or society (Table 19). Four per cent played golf regularly compared with only one Englishman: golf is somewhat a status symbol in America, as in some other countries, and it is significant that these lived on the three more-expensive subdivisions. Many reasons may be advanced to explain the popularity of games in the United States. Americans have more money to use for amusements; walking exercise is difficult to obtain unless one belongs to a golf club, for reasons explained already; there are a great number of golf courses and clubs; land is cheaper; everybody has a car; many professional associations and most masonic chapters form golf clubs.

Nine-pin bowling alleys are found in English works clubs and many public houses, especially country pubs, and in some localities the game is extremely popular. It has not attained the kind of mass popularity the ten-pin alleys have in the United States. (Why did they have to add another pin?[1]) There, whole families belong and there are clubs and groups for all ages; play goes on against a background of soft music with a restaurant to round off a pleasant evening out. The American-type of ten-pin bowling alley has been introduced to Great Britain and we may see changes in the activity in the future although no great enthusiasm for the sport has shown yet. Five Americans regularly went bowling but no Englishman.

Three American families belonged to a yacht club with premises on the Scioto River where a series of dams create large smooth expanses of water. Four other families possessed their own boat, with outboard motor, which they towed behind their car for family holidays and weekends. Two of these maintained a cottage on Lake Erie where the boats were kept

[1] The story is that a puritanical State legislature once prohibited ninepins as a time-wasting and frivolous game. So the players just added a tenth pin, and kept within the law.

most of the summer. The pastime of sailing and boating which has spread so rapidly across the United States is becoming increasingly popular in Great Britain but it is still a pursuit of the relatively well-to-do and only one of our English families possessed a boat, a sailing yacht, which they kept on the tidal Avon, at Bristol. In America, only householders with sizeable incomes, say, $8,000 (£2,857) and above, per annum, appeared able to indulge in the sport however; this income bracket includes the foreman and better-paid artisans, and most skilled professionals from school teachers upwards.

Several artisans on the lowest-cost subdivisions went fishing and hunting (for deer) although only one belonged to a club. Hunting is controlled by State laws but there are many good hunting areas within easy reach by car of most parts of the United States. The longer holiday trips made by many families during the summer vacations are often enlivened by hunting expeditions. City dwellers who were raised on farms have no need to join rifle clubs to learn to shoot, they have merely to re-employ skills which most of them learn in childhood on the farm. Nevertheless, rifle clubs are popular although none of our householders belonged.

Women's Athletic Activity

Four American housewives belonged to a gym club they had formed with a half a dozen other women on one subdivision. Membership of a yacht club was a family affair and women shared the sport. No women belonged to swimming clubs but the majority were able to swim and those with school-age children accompanied their offspring to the baths with great frequency in the summer. Every school seemed to own or have the major use of a swimming bath and family membership was possible. Every permanent summer camp, of which there are thousands in the United States, has its open-air swimming-pool and American children seem to take to water like the proverbial duck.

Adult Education and Cultural Organizations and Activities

No great interest was shown towards adult educational and

cultural activities in either country. Table 21 over- rather than under-estimates participation in this direction, since the majority of activities listed there refer to attendance no more than once a month to listen to a lecture or engage in conversation. With an occasional absence and the summer closure this could amount to only two or three attendances during the year. The music-appreciation society referred to already is an exception to this rule however.

TABLE 21

Educational and Cultural Organizations and Activities
(persons participating as per cent of the total sample)

	U.S.A.	England
Music Society	4	1
Discussion Group	4	—
League of Women Voters	2	—
Further Education classes	2	3
Miscellaneous education		
(coins, photography, art, ornithology)	4	3
Drama Society	—	1
Men attending at least one activity	6	6
Women attending at least one activity	8	1

Another society is interesting in that it illustrates the readiness with which Americans are prepared to submit to the discipline of a national organization. A few years ago, male close-harmony groups gained high popularity in one or two areas of the United States; they became known as 'barber shop' quartets. The fashion spread rapidly and a national 'Society for the Preservation and Encouragement of Barber Shop Singing in America' was formed and, today, every sizeable town has one or more 'chapters', a chapter comprising 30 to 50 groups each of which is registered with the national society. In Columbus there were two, the Buckeye Chapter with 65 groups and the Columbus Chapter with 100. Individual quartets tour the country singing at socials and concerts and appearing on radio and television programmes. A women's organization has now been set up.

The activities of the League of Women Voters will need explaining for English readers. This is a national organization, with branches in the large centres of population which are kept informed of political happenings, legislation in preparation and so on, at national and local level. Meetings are held, usually monthy, by the branches at which speakers lead discussions on interesting political subjects. An annual national delegate meeting is arranged. At elections each candidate is sent a standardized list of significant questions. The answers of rival candidates are published in parallel columns. A candidate may decline to reply but must use the prescribed outline of enquiries if he co-operates.

Thirty English families said that they attended a theatre performance very occasionally, i.e. for a special purpose like a birthday celebration. Only one was a regular theatre-goer. Bristol has two theatre companies, a large concert hall, and a variety theatre where occasional plays are presented. In Columbus, there are at least three large concert halls at two of which, on the university campus, regular programmes of plays and musical presentation are put on. A little over a quarter, i.e. 28, of the Americans we interviewed said they attended these occasionally. Fourteen attended a summer theatre under canvas, which operated during the four summer months a couple of miles away from our three higher-priced subdivisions. The number who said that they attended some theatre performance in the city was similar in the two countries. One gained the impression that, with one or two exceptions, for instance, 'I have been to the theatre in Bristol three times in 18 months', most of the English householders were indulging in wishful thinking. They had attended shows more or less regularly when living in town but since moving out to their present, peripheral, neighbourhood they had been prevented from doing so by a number of influences: cost, longer journey and poor public transport facilities, the difficulty of finding a baby-sitter and the cosiness of a 'home of our own' with the new television set. Fewer American families suffered these handicaps, and friends often met in town for a visit to a theatre usually preceded by a meal in a restaurant; this is part of the pattern of middle-class American life.

It would be uncharitable to leave music at this point without saying that, in both countries, a small minority said with one of their number, 'I love good music.' Unfortunately this gentleman qualified his expression by adding, 'I've seen "Oklahoma" five times because I love the music.'

Cinemas

Only 7 per cent English and 3 per cent American husbands and/or wives visited the cinema regularly. For many families, attending the cinema was something they did when they were courting or when there was a good film especially suitable for the children. 'If there is a nice show for the kids anywhere, I go.' The drive-in cinemas are patronized mainly by parents taking their children on a summer evening, or by courting couples—or so my wife and I were told when we proposed going to see a drive-in movie.

Libraries

Three-quarters of all American families used their local library compared with one-third of all English families; except on private-enterprise estates, where the proportion was one-half, the proportions were distributed fairly evenly over the various neighbourhoods. It must not be concluded from these figures that American *adults* are great readers and English adults are not. The provision of children's books and reading-room facilities in the Worthington, Columbus, library was far superior to anything English libraries have to offer; we found that American mothers started using the local library for picture books and literature suited to 3- and 4-year-olds. This habit the children quite clearly continued into the teenage period. Many high-school youngsters did their homework in the comfortable, and quiet, air-conditioned, library reading-room.

Many complaints were registered by English households about the lack, or poor quality, of the local library. A number of the newcomers had been used to the superior city library and were meeting county provision for the first time. 'The estate is large enough to have its own library,' said one man who was studying for a technical examination. 'The library is too far away or I might have belonged,' said another. This man, a professional engineer, owned a car and the library was little more than a mile away: it seems reasonable to suppose that he was trying to excuse his failure to use a service which he felt he ought to have done. Perhaps he was not quite so honest as two others of his neighbours: the first said, 'We are not great readers. Is there one (i.e. a library)?' and the second, 'I've got no time with the car and garden to look after as well.'

'Do we use the library? No, not since we've had television', describes the situation in many English homes. In many more the habit of reading was never acquired in early childhood. The American kind of enthusiastic thirsting for knowledge seems not to be shared by many English children or, it would seem, their parents. 'We buy magazines, but I haven't got time to look at them'; this remark would never have been passed by an American housewife. She must keep up to date with her reading of magazines like *Time* and the *Saturday Evening Post*, or she would lose status with her friends for she would be unable to enter so earnestly into the interminable discussions which American women appear to enjoy so much when they get together in groups.

General

In breaking down adult leisure activities into sections, as we have done, above, we have been able to show the greater variety available to the Americans, and the slender opportunities open to Englishmen, when they move into a new neighbourhood. We have not been able to show what this means to the individual. To try to correct this we thought it would be interesting to compare the leisure activities of two working-class households, one in each country. As far as English families were concerned, the task was nigh impossible for few had any real pattern of social life outside the home. A visit to the pub or a club to play darts once in a while and that was that. The wife had her sewing and, if she was lucky, the 'telly'. One said he played darts with a friend at Longwell Green, an adjacent neighbourhood, and sometimes his friend visited them for the same purpose. Another went occasionally to the works' club for a game of snooker, darts or table tennis. His wife belonged to no outside activity: 'If I joined anything it would be an evening class,' she said. The first man was 30 years of age and his wife 26: the second was 33 and his wife 26 years; all had left school at 14 years of age. The household incomes were £11 ($76) and £8 ($55) weekly, respectively. Neither had a car or motor cycle. The first journeyed to work by bus which took him an hour each way. The second walked to work.

The pattern of life for working-class members on our lowest-cost American subdivision differed markedly from the above. The following actual description is not untypical of many others: the husband is 26 years of age and his wife is 27 years. They have three children, 3½ years, 2 years and 5 months old. He is a factory worker earning $112 a week (£40) take-home pay. They own a three-year-old Ford which is left at home for the wife to drive when she needs it to go shopping or to visit friends, i.e. a couple of times a week. Their home is ten minutes' walk from the bus line (route) and the wife drives her husband to the bus-stop in the morning if she needs to retain the car for the day. He may get a lift home in the evening for you never pass an acquaintance who is walking without offering him a lift. He belongs to his firm's sports club and plays baseball in the summer and basket-ball in the winter, usually one evening a week. His wife looks after the three children, does the shopping in the car a couple of times a week. She attends a school club once a month and, again, on an average, once a month she plays bridge with members of a card group. If it is hot summer weather she will take the children to the swimming-pool having 'called' a friend on the telephone and arranged to meet her there.

English readers may feel that a specially-active American family has been selected. This is not the case. The majority of working-class families can afford to pursue this kind of recreational pattern of life and enjoy doing so. The average English husband when he comes home after a day's work will more likely say, as did one, when asked to what social organizations he be-

longed, 'None. We've got enough to do bringing up the children. We have to break up the garden and then we relax to
television.' In fact, both he and his wife belonged to the local
Church—but attended on Sundays only. After he has had a
meal and rested he may 'potter' ('putter' to an American)
round the garden or go up to the pub for a drink. In England
these are pleasurable occupations after a day's work. In the
humid heat of a Middle West summer evening my wife and I
found it more attractive to seek the relative comfort indoors
where an outsized fan, two feet six inches in diameter, helped
to reduce the sensation of heat and where the window screens
kept the mosquitoes at bay. These conditions extend over most
of central and eastern United States throughout the summer
months.

Whether the Englishman would want to do more if he received the American standard of remuneration, or possessed
the mobility provided by an American car and petrol at 3*s*. a
gallon, is questionable. The habit of belonging to organizations
begins in early childhood in America as the chapter on children
and young people shows. In every extra-curricular school activity the child is taught to take his share in the government of the
organization or activity. This grounding in committee procedure
and group action becomes second nature and the school or college experience is automatically recalled when, in later life, he
meets a situation which calls for organization. Instead of saying
'They ought to do something', 'They ought to provide a community centre', as our English householders repeated so often,
the American gets on with the job and sets up an organization
to fill the gap by voluntary effort, at minimum cost, albeit with
the expenditure of much time but accompanied by the promotion of a great deal of friendliness. It appeared to us out-
siders that a great deal of time was wasted in some of these
activities and, to quote the remarks of one, an American minister, on this subject who wrote in a private letter, 'Some people
get so involved in social activities, oftentime very trivial and
not at all satisfying or involving deep emotional involvement,
that their time is fully taken up . . . that they resent giving up
time—some are physically unable—to help in Church work.'
This may well be true of middle-class residents in the United

179

States. It was not noticeably true of the working-class members or of the younger age-groups. It would not be at all true of conditions in England where, as we show in Chapter 10, a much smaller proportion of the population is involved in Church activity.

In spite of these minor criticisms of the American social way of life we were left with the conviction that many newcomers on English estates would have welcomed, and have greatly bene-fited from, the quick friendliness and enthusiasm for social organization observed by us on most subdivisions in the United States. In fact, 10 per cent of all English households stated that more clubs (or associations) were needed. It is significant, how-ever, that only one added '. . . but that's up to us'. The others expected someone else to supply the initiative.

12

SUMMING UP: FACTS, FACTORS
AND THE FUTURE

Facts

UNDOUBTEDLY, the most noticeable contrast between
the two countries to emerge from the enquiry is the
greater neighbourliness existing on American subdivisions contrasted with the aloofness, if not actual chilliness,
which passes for neighbourliness on English estates, both council
and private-enterprise. Yet, surprisingly, in both countries
there was general agreement that neighbours are best kept at
arm's length: only rarely should you make real friends of your
neighbours.

In both countries, the great majority, some 80 per cent, were
very content with the house and neighbourhood they had
chosen. But for many Americans this was recognized to be only
a short-time satisfaction: it was accepted that in a few years
the family would be moving on.

In the choice of a new neighbourhood both groups of
nationals rated highly its accessibility relative to the husband's
place of work. English householders, council and private-enterprise, rated more highly the nearness of open country, a feature
which weighed with Americans not at all. The latter sought
a good school system: this was not mentioned by English
people.

Many women on English estates experienced loneliness. They
missed the friends from whom their move to the new neighbourhood had separated them. No loneliness was evident on
American subdivisions. All families were able to keep in touch

with friends and relatives in other parts of the city with little difficulty. Many kept in close, frequent, contact with friends in other towns, some at a great distance by English standards.

On all English neighbourhoods there were complaints of too few organizations for adults and, especially, too few for children. No English organization, religious or secular, appeared to be adequately equipped to welcome newcomers or to recruit them to their membership. In America, there were many formal and informal organizations whose activities, consciously or unconsciously, helped to make newcomers feel at home in their new neighbourhood.

In both countries, children proved to be very important in bringing parents, especially mothers, together for neighbourly intercourse. In America, this applied particularly to extracurricular school activities and youth organizations like the Scouts and 4-H club. In England, these organizations were relatively unimportant.

American Churches provide a wealth of social club facilities for all ages—for children, teenagers and adults of both sexes— as well as programmes for religious instruction and observance. English Churches concentrate on the religious aspects of their faith and few arrange purely social functions for their members. In America, churchgoing was especially important on higher-priced subdivisions and relatively unimportant on low-cost subdivisions. In England, only a small minority of the families interviewed were churchgoers.

Englishmen of all income levels appeared more educated to an appreciation of the need to conserve natural beauty in the countryside. They were also most alert to the concomitant danger of uncontrolled development. Most Americans, on the other hand, appeared to be living cosily in the belief that both natural beauty and land suitable for development were inexhaustible and expendable. It is true, of course, that they have more land to spread themselves over, but the Americans we met showed little awareness of the unpleasant corollaries of longer daily journeys to work and recession of the natural environment from daily living which are applicable however much land you have to build on. For most, a new motor road and another and a bigger, faster automobile were complete solutions to bigger and bigger towns. We met little more than half a dozen, during the whole of our stay in America, who appeared to have given serious thought to this problem. These few lived near the more congested eastern seaboard.

Factors

Americans are at all times vitally interested in what goes on around them: they appear more alive: they are ready to make mistakes: they are not worried about the possibility of being snubbed or made to feel uncomfortable: they are not prepared to stay at home feeling miserable and blaming someone else for shortcomings in neighbourhood services or organization. If something or some service is needed they shout about it, set up an organization and in no time the gap has been filled—usually by private voluntary enterprise. Too often, English householders, who were quick to point to inadequacies, appeared quite content to do no more than moan about the dilatoriness of the local authority or an unenterprising direction of a local or national voluntary society. This contrast of attitude we concluded from our investigations was very largely the result of environment, education, training and upbringing. A factor that may be operative, however, is the survival in England of the aristocratic tradition: the reliance of the lower- and middle-class English person on some upper-class person always to take the initiative. Evidence of this is to be found in the hereditary titles and acquired honours which appear beside the names of presidents and vice-presidents of most voluntary bodies.

By contrast, we have shown that in the United States children are trained from the age of 12 or so onwards to take active part in the organization and leadership of school and voluntary leisure activities: that mothers are prepared to set up groups and clubs for educational, child welfare and leisure pursuits: that to an American male a problem is a challenge, and for every problem a solution can and must be found—quickly. We met this outlook nowhere in England.

In solving problems associated with removal of residence the American starts with a number of distinct advantages. In every new neighbourhood in which he arrives he finds a sizeable nucleus of families which has had experience of other removals. This nucleus comprises, or at least includes, people who recognize the value of getting acquainted with one's neighbours quickly. The Churches and the secular voluntary organizations of America have been coping with shifts of vast numbers of people for many decades. They have arranged their policies and streamlined their activities to take notice of newcomers, immediately. Experience has shown them that speed is essential in order to achieve the maximum impact. In a more static society, such as has obtained throughout much of England until quite recently, leadership is determined by birth or by slow natural selection: the sense of belonging is inborn or only gradually acquired. In a rapidly changing society, on the other hand, if loneliness is to be prevented, if neighbourliness is to be sustained, if social organizations are to flourish, a framework has to be provided for newcomers to establish status, for new leaders to be identified quickly, for everybody to acquire the sense of belonging in a very short space of time. American society has recognized and makes provision for this: English society does not.

We have seen that Americans are infinitely more mobile. They move from town to town and neighbourhood to neighbourhood more frequently, and with little apparent disturbance to their equanimity. Every family has at least one automobile and little dependence is placed on public transport. Social satisfaction can be achieved both on and off the home neighbourhood with little personal travelling inconvenience.

American incomes are, relatively, much higher than English incomes, job for job. American homemakers have much more free time during the day thanks to more comprehensive household equipment. They not only have more time for bridge-clubs and Church circles, they also have more money in their purses to pay for gasoline for the car they use, fees for the nursery class, subscriptions to the discussion group, payment for the baby-sitter and for the purchase of food for parties.

The influence of climate on way of life in the two countries is difficult adequately to assess. But, one can say that the long hot American summer drives people out on to the back porch if not into the yard where we discovered hoards of flying insects

lie in wait for the taste of English blood,[1] whereas the uncer-
tainty of the English summer tends frequently to drive the
English family indoors. This could encourage them to devote
more time to morning 'coffees' and indoor 'partying' but it
does not; lack of experience and a tradition of suspicion of
neighbours appear too strong.

Whilst they had a great deal more to do with their neighbours, and partly for this very reason, Americans were more
concerned about preserving their privacy. The factors which
have been shown to have bearing on this are the open layout
of the yards, the invitation to informal coffee sessions and so
on. The fact that English families indulge less in these get-
togethers, and that invariably one of their first actions on taking
up residence in a new house is to fence in the garden, makes
them less vulnerable to invasion of privacy.

Future

It is always hazardous in assessing sociological research to attempt to forecast the future. Nevertheless, trends are observable
in England, at the present time, which suggest that many of the
features of present-day American everyday life will be adopted
by English families during the next decade or so. The most
noticeable, and in some ways most disturbing, of these features
is the increase in personal mobility which is making its way
rapidly down the social and income scales in England. It is
safe to forecast that in ten years' time every English family,
where the head of the family is 50 years of age or less, will have
a motor-car for its own use. This will leave only some elderly
households entirely dependent upon public transport or the
cars of their friends and relatives. In ten years' time every young
family man will automatically put a sizeable slice of the expected 3 or 4 per cent increase in real income per annum
towards buying and running a car. This is happening now.
It has represented a major revolution in the way of life of ordinary people many of whom ten years ago never dreamed of

[1] One returned Englishman wrote in *The Listener*: 'The odd thing was that
nobody ever seemed to sit out of doors or potter about or do anything except drive
off to work; on Sundays they did come out but only to drive their power-mowers
up and down the lawns' (John Rosselli, 'A Frontier Suburb', Jan. 3, 1963).

owning a car. There will be a further decline in public transport service. This will hit hardest the older people without cars but will also in some areas affect women during the day-time and teenagers at all times unless and until the two-car family becomes the rule or father shows himself more co-operative than at present in forming car pools for the journey to work. The increasing difficulty of parking in urban centres may ultimately force him to do so. Some of my colleagues of my own generation do not believe that the factors to compensate for the decline in public transport services, present in the United States, will develop to anything like the same extent in the United Kingdom in the foreseeable future. I do not agree with them. Public transport services are withdrawn because people do not use them and the most important factor in this is the increase in the car-owning population. As still more services disappear the greater will be the urge to afford a car. As roads become more congested and as more English people spend their holidays abroad and learn to appreciate the value of good motor roads, the need for more motor roads and better parking facilities everywhere—in town and village—will be appreciated. At the moment, England is behind almost every nation in western Europe. This could change in a decade. Indeed, it must.

People who buy houses on new estates in England are mainly in their late twenties or early thirties. Because they all will have a family car, when they move they will, like Americans today, be able to maintain old friendships, and seek new ones, off the estate and away from the neighbourhood. They will have more money to spend on entertainment, including subscriptions to social organizations. Housewives will have more pocket money to buy household gadgets which should increase their leisure: they will find more money and time to devote to entertaining both in and out of the home. The last few years —again following American trends—have seen the growth of coffee bars, 'sea food' cafés and Chinese restaurants. In England there is a new interest in eating. When we first penned these lines we wrote: this has not noticeably spread to social organizations but it could well do so with more pre-packed, prepared and frozen foods, and with more money to spend on them: American partying habits in home and institution could

follow. As we revise the chapter, a year later, we can add that
we have since learnt that in our private-enterprise survey areas,
a Women's Institute, a Townswomen's Guild and several
women's chapel groups have organized morning 'get-togethers',
for little groups of members, at which coffee and cakes are
dispensed in private homes in order to raise funds for special
projects. Apparently, American female partying habits have
already arrived.

The Englishman's house is still his castle. Only carefully
chosen guests are invited in. The dimensions of his sitting
room(s) are, in the main, based on family use. The modern
American home is planned to accommodate parties of up to
30 guests and its kitchen designed to provide refreshment for
these large numbers with speed. Few present-day English
sitting-rooms and kitchens could cope with family entertainment on the American scale. But developers of higher-priced
houses in England are already providing larger sitting-rooms
and more spacious kitchens to cater for clients who want to
provide cheese-and-wine evenings for their friends, to hold
bridge parties and the like. It does not need much imagination
to see that, as incomes rise and leisure time increases, the demands for similar facilities will come from those lower down the
income scale who at present have neither the money nor the
experience to crave them.

During the last two or three years, since our interviews were
made, community centres and women's clubs have been set up
on new peripheral estates around Bristol: they are thriving as
never before. There is a greater demand for organized social
activity than the southern half of the county of Gloucestershire
has ever experienced. People are coming out of their homes.
They show that they want to mix with one another. We have
seen confusion and frustration for few English families have the
experience of organizing voluntary activity on the scale of the
American families which we studied. The Churches are relatively unimportant as centres of social activity: hence a different
pattern of social activity is emerging: one based on the community centre, the Further Education class and the Women's
Institute or the Townswomen's Guild. So far, in general, men
have tended to lag behind women in this social surge: Women's

Institutes have flourished but British Legion Clubs declined. More money, mobility and leisure, together with more education, in the broadest sense, could alter this, although even in America it was noticeable that men lagged behind women in the drive for social activity.

Finally, mobility as to residence. The full extent of the changes in mental outlook and in the pattern of everyday life which take place when a family acquires its first car have not been explored by sociologists. We have shown that American families move from town to town and neighbourhood to neighbourhood with relative ease:[1] that they maintain old friendships when they do so because travel by car is so easy. Ten years ago, the Bristol Corporation found it well-nigh impossible to get families in urgent need of housing accommodation to accept a house ten miles from the centre of the city at the end of an hour-long bus ride. In the same neighbourhood today, private-enterprise houses are selling faster than the builders can erect them. For many of these newcomers, a newly-acquired car eats up the ten miles to work, to relatives and to old friends. These young professional and skilled artisan families are happy to move out 'into the country' as they view the rural-urban fringe. More will do so and they will be joined by the, at present, lower-income groups as car ownership expands. In the last twelve months, two new dormitory town-suburbs of 20,000 population each, separated from Bristol by the green belt, have been proposed by planning authorities, one in Gloucestershire and one in Somerset. One of our survey neighbourhoods lies in a third such. All these three 'new towns' as they are being mis-called are within 12 miles of the centre of the city. Most of the houses on them will be built by private enterprise.

Meanwhile, content in the belief that working-class families will not willingly leave the old familiar home surroundings, English city councils engaged in the clearance of worn-out urban neighbourhoods are urgently pursuing programmes of flat (apartment) building of 10 to 20 storeys. They produce im-

[1] Not only can you hire a car in one town and return it in another, a thousand miles away, but you can do the same with a truck (lorry) or trailer; these last are as big as a small English delivery van. This service, provided by firms with nation-wide networks, enormously simplifies removals for American families, all of whom possess at least one large car capable of towing a large trailer load.

pressive-looking plans and assiduously woo business concerns to develop the worn-out hearts of their cities as modern shopping and recreational centres. They discount or ignore the fact that down-town shopping centres of American provincial cities are dead—killed by the changed habits of a car-owning population which prefers the 'comfort' of marketing in the urban-fringe shopping plaza to the scramble for parking space in the centre of the city. 'It can never happen here,' they imply. But can it not? At Yate, one of our survey areas, a shopping centre project on the American model has been proposed within the last year; as planned, it is on a scale which would be large enough to draw custom from the city.

In the future it is clear to some of us that English rural-urban fringe areas can expect to receive more and more families from humbler and humbler homes—each owning a family car: the new neighbourhoods will contain an increasing number of people who have come from other, more-distant, towns, as the working population savours the luxury of greater freedom of choice of job and residential neighbourhood with which the motor car endows them. For the same reason, each new family may be expected to view the change of residence with less permanence than the newcomers of past decades. This means that new estates and new neighbourhoods will be settled by different sorts of people: newcomers who have no roots locally and, maybe, will not put down permanent roots at all: but newcomers notwithstanding: people with no inbred loyalty to the district, the club or the community, who will, nevertheless, because they have more leisure and more money in their pockets, want to engage in neighbourly activities partly in order to make new friends and acquaintances, and some perhaps to satisfy a need to establish a position in the 'pecking order' of the neighbourhood. In England, as we have seen, too few avenues for meeting neighbours and making friends exist today. Some of the older organizations, especially in rural areas, are still regarded as preserves of the long-time residents. This attitude of mind is changing: it will do so still more rapidly over the next decade.

In the south Gloucestershire fringe to the north of Bristol, the last two or three years have seen community centre after community centre established, each with its full-time warden whose salary is paid by the County Council: there are now eight where ten years ago there was none. Each community centre has a wide range of activities, from serious discussion to 'pop' music. Some of the Free Churches are engaged in extensive building programmes. The county youth service has never had so many youth clubs on its books or so many applications for grants in aid of buildings. Townswomen's Guilds and Women's Institutes have bulging membership rolls. Yet, seemingly, these developments are still not enough to cope with the present demand. A short while ago an organizer from the National Association of Women's Clubs visited a number of working-class estates with the area officer of the Gloucestershire Community Council. They found many women longing for an opportunity to get together just to talk to one another: they were working-class women who were awed with the rather ambitious (to them) talks of a well-run Townswomen's Guild or were put off by the intimacy of the Mothers' Union. As we write, two months later, there are five Women's Clubs meeting regularly for talk and tea: their programmes contain little else at present but they are extremely popular with the working-class women who attend.[1]

The moral of the last paragraph—and indeed the message of this enquiry—seems to be that, in the future, new rural fringe neighbourhoods may expect to see demands for bigger, better and more comprehensive patterns of social activity and participation. Those concerned with the organization and administration of social activities, and in this we include the Churches if they decide to pay more attention to social activity, can look forward to a period of expansion and, if they plan their programmes wisely, could build up an entirely new social pattern in these urban peripheries, one which is neither rural nor urban. Failure to plan for this kind of development would lead to a great deal of frustration amongst the adult newcomers which could in time infect their children and lead to further increases in juvenile problems and delinquency. Past failure to promote a particular organization or develop an existing activity in a

[1] Stop press news is that the five clubs are arranging a conference where they can meet together to further friendship and discuss problems.

certain locality cannot be read as a barometer of future possibilities and should not be used as an excuse for inactivity: the recent successful records of the Women's Clubs, above, and of some parent–teachers' associations, elsewhere, demonstrate this. We must repeat that the people moving to new estates today are different in many important respects from those who moved out before the war. At present, they may have fewer cars and refrigerators than their American cousins but they are more akin to them than they know in their needs and aspirations. Unfortunately, in some new English neighbourhoods, in the tight little social groups, 'newcomer' is still a term of disparagement. We believe it will not remain so and that 'newcomer' will become, as in the United States, an open sesame to the social activities of the Church and of secular organizations in more and more new neighbourhoods.

APPENDIX A

INTERVIEW OUTLINE

(Sections relevant to the subject of the book)

A   1. Date of taking up residence in present home.
     2. Neighbourhoods previously lived in since marriage: status (householder or rooms): length of time resident in each.
     3. What other neighbourhoods were considered when latest move was made?
     4. Consideration given to future moves.

B   Details of present accommodation
     1. Tenure.
     2. Type of house.
     3. Rooms: number and type.
     4. Garage, carport.
     5. Type of street or road: main, side, cross street, court, cul-de-sac.
     6. Dimensions of plot (lot).

C   1. Reasons for choosing the present neighbourhood.
     2. If given free choice which neighbourhood would have been chosen and why?
     3. Present links or ties with the city: friends, relatives, work, shopping, recreation etc: frequency of visit.

D   1. The limits of the neighbourhood as given by the householder.
     2. Are people of the neighbourhood of the same kind or do they differ?
     3. If they differ, in what way? Income, occupation, class origin (no leads given).
     4. How many neighbours are known by name?
     5. What sort of neighbours have the family?
     6. Definition of a good neighbour.

E   1. How would the neighbourhood be rated as a place to live in: excellent, good, fair, poor? Reasons.
     2. Any wish to move to another neighbourhood now. Name of the neighbourhood. Reasons for wishing to move. What neighbourhoods would be avoided and the reasons for this?

F   Transportation
     1. Vehicles owned by the household. Persons who drive them.
     2. The husband's/wife's journey to work: means of transport used.

G   Present house
   1. What is especially liked about it?
   2. What is especially disliked about it?

H   1. Services and facilities, and their location, used by the household: school, church, parks, libraries, clinics, shops; professional services of doctor and dentist, cinemas, theatres, concert halls, clubs and societies.
   2. Details as to their use, and accessibility.
   3. Services lacking in the neighbourhood which the family thinks should be available.

I   Husband's (and wife's where applicable) employment
   1. Occupation(s).
   2. Location of work place: length of time employed there: any change since taking up residence.
   3. Workmates living close by. Number. How well known.
   4. Time of journey to work. Is this longer or shorter than before the move to the neighbourhood?
   5. Means of transport: self driven by car, motorcycle, cycle: by bus or train: car pool: wife drives: walk.

J   Personal data
   1. Age.
   2. Education and/or training of husband and wife.
   3. Income.
   4. Age and sex of children: school: future education aimed at.

K   Household payments
   1. Rent or loan repayments (including tax and insurances).
   2. Utilities: gas (winter and summer): electricity (winter and summer), water, telephone.

L   Household equipment
   1. Radio, television, record player, piano.
   2. Automatic washer, automatic drier, vacuum cleaner, sewing machine, refrigerator, deep freeze, power lawn mower.
   3. Sink disposal unit, air conditioner, attic fan.

M   Evident needs and/or frustrations.

APPENDIX B

CHURCH COMMITTEES OF AMERICAN CHURCHES

A. KING AVENUE METHODIST CHURCH, COLUMBUS, OHIO[1]

Board of Trustees
For a period of 3 years — 9 persons; 1 acts as Chairman
3 new ones elected each year

(These are rotated and only serve for 3 consecutive years)

Stewards	Elected for 3 years: 43 active members
Membership and Evangelism	7 elected members, Membership Chairman of the Women's Society for Christian Service, President of Senior M.Y.F., Church School Secretary
Education	9 members elected, Pastoral Assistant or Christian Education Director, Church School Dept., Heads of Representative for Youth, Representative for Adults, Librarian
Missions	6 elected members, Secretary of Missionary Education of Women's Society for Christian Service
Finance	9 elected members, Treasurer, Assistant Treasurer, Financial Secretary, Lay Leader, Women's Society for Christian Service, Treasurer
Nominating Committee	9 elected members
Pastoral Relations and Pulpit Supply Committee	9 elected members
Records and History	3 elected members
Wills and Legacies	6 elected members, Chairman of Finance Committee

[1] The information concerning King Avenue Methodist Church was kindly supplied by Mr. R. Bernhagen.

194

Music Committee	9 elected members
Church Property Committee	8 elected members, Treasurer, President of Women's Society for Christian Service, Chairman of Board of Trustees
Christian Vocations Committee	5 elected, Pastoral Assistant or Christian Education Director
Communion Stewards	9 elected members
Hospital and Homes	3 elected members
Audit	3 elected members
Investment	7 elected members
Good Literature	3 elected members, Women's Society for Christian Service, Secretary of Literature, Church Librarian
Arrangements and Decorating	5 elected couples
Women's Society for Christian Service	7 circles; each select own leader and officers
Choir	50–60 members

B. LINWORTH METHODIST CHURCH, COLUMBUS, OHIO[1]

Board of Trustees	9 members: Chairman, Vice-Chairman, Recording Secretary
Total Church Membership	Adults 350
Official Board	9 Elective Stewards, Lay Leader, Church School Superintendent, Representative of Methodist Union, Lay Member of Conference, Reserve Lay Member of Conference, Director of Stewardship, Lay Speaker, Communion Steward, Recording Steward, District Steward, Reserve District Steward, Treasurer, Financial Secretary, Chairman of Commission on Membership and Evangelism, Chairman of Commission on Education, Chairman of Commission on Steward-

[1] The information concerning Linworth Methodist Church was kindly supplied by Mr. R. Linville.

195

Official Board (*contd.*)

ship and Finance, Chairman of Commission on Missions, Chairman of Parsonage Committee, Chairman of Music Committee. (The Chairman of the Official Board is the Lay Leader, Secretary is the Recording Steward.)

Committees

Membership and Evangelism

9 members, Chairman, Recording Secretary

Education

9 members, Chairman, Recording Secretary

Stewardship and Finance

10 members, Chairman, Recording Secretary

Missions

6 members, Chairman, Recording Secretary

Pastoral Relations Committee

5 members, Chairman, Recording Secretary

Parsonage Committee

5 members, Chairman, Recording Secretary

Music Committee

4 members, Chairman, Recording Secretary

Committee on Adult

5 members, Chairman, Recording Secretary

Committee on Church Policy

Lay Leader, Church School Superintendent, Chairman of Commission on Membership and Evangelism, Chairman of Commission on Education, Chairman of Commission on Stewardship and Finance, Chairman of Commission on Missions, Chairman of Board of Trustees, President of Women's Society of Christian Service, President of Methodist's Men's Club, President of Senior High Methodist Youth Fellowship

Nomination Committee

6 members, Pastor

Choir

President, Librarian, Telephone Chairman

Newsletter

Editor, 2 Assistants

Senior Methodist Youth Fellowship	16 members, President, Vice-President, Secretary, Treasurer, News Reporter, Faith Chairman, Citizenship Chairman, Witness Chairman, Outreach Chairman, Fellowship Chairman, Calling Chairman, 4 advisors
Intermediate Methodist Youth Fellowship	President, Vice-President, Secretary, Treasurer, 4 advisors
Methodist Men's Club	President, Vice-President, Secretary, Treasurer
Women's Society of Christian Service	60 members, President, Vice-President, Secretary, Treasurer, Chairman Missionary Education, Chairman of Promotion, Chairman of Spiritual Life, Chairman of Children, Chairman of Youth and Student, Chairman of Local Church Activities, Chairman of Christian Social Relations, Chairman of Supply, Chairman of Literature and Publications

C. BETHEL METHODIST CHURCH, LINWORTH, COLUMBUS, OHIO[1]

Nature of the Church	Bethel Church is Methodist in denomination. It is presently located in a rapidly developing suburb of Columbus, Ohio. It is a small Church numbering at present 350 members which means real contact with some 140 families. Formal membership means children 12 years and older and adults. It has an annual budget of approximately 15,000 dollars (£5,357) a year met primarily by approximately 100 pledges averaging about 120 dollars (£42) a pledge a year. The following persons who receive a salary for their services: Minister: full time, salary $5,000 (£1,785) plus rent, free parsonage Choir Director: part time $40 (£14) per month

---

[1] The information concerning Bethel Methodist Church was kindly supplied by the Reverend Elford Hoff.

Nature of the Church (*contd.*)	Secretary: part time $35 per month Custodian: part time $1,200 (£428) per year
Board of Trustees	Official Board
Official Board	Education Commission, Membership Commission, Finance Commission, Missions Commission, Social Relations Commission
Commissions	These groups carry on the basic work of the Church
Education	(Most important sub-group in the Church) Chairman (Sunday School Superintendent) appoints the teachers, keeps the Sunday School in operation. Vice-Chairman and Assistant Chairman. Secretary: keeps records, orders materials and supplies. Treasurer: receives the offerings, pays the bills, handles about 1,200 dollars (£428) a year. Sunday School Teachers: 24 teachers with 18 classes meeting weekly including 4 adult classes: average attendance at Sunday School 180. Senior High Methodist Youth Fellowship: a group for 15–18-year-olds. This group has its officers as well as 2 adult advisors: it meets on Sunday night. Junior High Methodist Youth Fellowship: a group for 12–15-year-olds. It has its own officers with adult advisors and meets on Sunday night. Young Adult Group: this group meets once a month in the evening. It is a group for adults in their 30s: very active. President, Vice-President, Secretary, Treasurer handles 600 dollars a year. Older Adult Group: meets about 4 times a year, President, Vice-President.
Membership and Evangelism	Meets monthly. There is a Chairman and about 5 teams of visitors. Every other month they make calls in the homes of non-church people. There are periodic dinner and training sessions for new members in the fellowship.

Finance	Has charge of raising money for the Church. Supervises a major fund visitation every year to every family. Chairman. Treasurer who writes the cheques for the Church. Financial Secretary who receives and deposits the contributions.
Missions	Supervises raising of funds for Mission giving Chairman. Meets only occasionally.
Christian Social Relations Commission	Holds forums on ethical and political issues. Chairman.

Committees under the Official Board directly

Music Committee	Chairman: has charge of choirs and purchase of music. It meets occasionally.
Parsonage Committee	Chairman: keeps the parsonage in repair. Uses much volunteer help to paint, paper, etc.
Pastoral Relations Committee	Chairman: supervises the relationship between the Pastor and the Congregation.
Building Committee	Chairman, Vice-Chairman, Secretary. This committee supervises the planning for future needs in land and building. At Bethel presently a very important committee.

Authorised Groups not Directly Supervised by the Official Board:

Women's Society of Christian Service	Meets as a general group. President, Chairman and Representative Church organizations. Vice-President: in charge of programme. Secretary, Treasurer handles 1,200 dollars (£428) a year. Membership Chairman: sends cards for meetings and makes calls for new members. Christian social relations. Raises charity funds. Sponsors study course. Spiritual Life: arranges Devotions. Youth Division: helps with youth work. Local Church Activities Chairman: sponsors Church suppers. Missions Chairman: once a year study group of 4 sessions.

Appendix B

Two Choirs	One junior and one senior. Paid director for senior choir. A voluntary director for junior choir. Choir practice weekly.
Boy Scouts	Cub Pack. Ages 9–12. Older boys go to another Church. Two adult advisors from our Church.
Mother's Club	President, Vice-President, Secretary; makes 'phone calls to old and potential new members. Treasurer; $1,200 (£428) is raised and spent. The Mother's Club meets monthly, sponsors many projects to help the Sunday School to raise money to provide volunteers to drive youngsters to the Church.
Men's Club	This group meets periodically: sponsors several affairs during the Church year such as Father-Son Banquet, etc. Contributes large amounts of voluntary help to keep the Church building in repair.
Baseball Team	In the summer the Church sponsors a very enthusiastic baseball team for men of the Church. Team Manager and Team Captain.
Play School Committee	Organizes a school 3 mornings a week for 3–5-year-olds. Chairman, Vice-Chairman, Secretary, Treasurer. Approximately 30 youngsters enrolled.
Yearly Events in the Church	Involve much work by the various groups and co-operation between them.

Yearly Events in the Church:

1. Homecoming: visitors and old friends come back for a dinner and a meeting.
2. Lenten Meetings: supper meetings followed by discussion and prayer meeting.
3. Camps and weekend outings; very important in the structure of the Church.
   Young adults—one weekend a year.
   Youth 15–18; one entire week, 8 adults help council.
   Youth 12–15: one entire week, 6 adults help council.

200

Yearly Events in the Church
(*contd.*)

4. Church-sponsored public suppers. The public is invited and Church members come and serve supper. All organizations co-operate. Usually a Church bazaar in connection with one supper a year where handwork of Church members is sold.

APPENDIX C

FRANKLIN COUNTY 4-H CLUB CAMP

June 21–28, 1959

JUNIOR CAMP

Opens at 2.00 p.m., June 21
Closes at 9.00 a.m., June 24

SENIOR CAMP

Opens at 9.00 a.m., June 24
Closes at 11.00 a.m., June 28

DAILY PROGRAM

6.30 a.m.	Reveille
7.00 a.m.	Flag Raising
7.15 a.m.	Breakfast
7.45 a.m.	Clean-up Time
8.15 a.m.	Group Meetings
9.00 a.m.	Crafts and Conservation[1]
10.00 a.m.	Swim Instruction and Crafts
11.00 a.m.	General Swim
12. Noon	Lunch
1.00 p.m.	Rest Period
1.30 p.m.	Conservation and Swim Instruction
2.30 p.m.	Organized Games—Hike—Archery
4.00 p.m.	General Swim
5.00 p.m.	Council Meeting
5.30 p.m.	Supper
6.30 p.m.	Group Meetings—Campfire
9.00 p.m.	Recreation
10.15 p.m.	Lights Out
10.30 p.m.	Taps

[1] Conservation includes nature study.

Appendix C

PERMANENT CAMP STAFF

Camp Manager	Bernard Druen
Assoc. Manager	Charles Younkman
Conservation	Worth Annan
Swimming	Barbara Hartcook
Cook	Marie Becker
Asst. Cooks	Carolyn Pittman, Evelyn Coleville

JUNIOR COUNSELLORS

Carolyn Gill	Julia Dobrune
Patti Kunz	Sally Andersen
Carolyn Strait	Nancy LaMoreaux
Harriet Linebaugh	Larry Hoffman
Elaine Lehnert	David Harper
Louise Bischoff	Joel Rogers
Cynthia Horn	Jim Smith
Marilyn Karrer	Harry Halliday
Marilyn Litzinger	Jeff Bockman
Linda Longshord	Phil Scott
Mary Lou Schwind	Robert Kaderly
Lang Borror	Jim Huggett
Susan Elner	

COUNTY STAFF

George B. Ganyard . . .	County Extension Agent, Agr.
Jim Mills	County Extension Agent, 4-H
Bertha Everhard	County Extension Agent, Home Ec.
Mrs. John Potts . . .	4-H Advisor
Mrs. L. E. Zimmer . .	4-H Advisor
Betty Bartholomew . .	County Bd. of Health Nurses
Ralph Tolbert	Ohio State University Graduate
Mr. & Mrs. Russell Boring . .	Groveport

4-H Camping offers a variety of experiences to the camper. We learn to live, work and play together. You are important in the camp life. The programme is planned to give you a happy experience.

While here at camp you will need to pitch in to do your share. With you doing your best to help out, we will have a good camp.

INDEX

205

Index